STORIES
Behind the

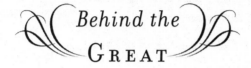

GREAT
TRADITIONS

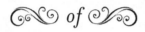

of

CHRISTMAS

Other Books by Ace Collins

STORIES
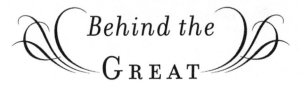
Behind the
GREAT
TRADITIONS
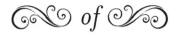
of
CHRISTMAS

ACE COLLINS

ILLUSTRATIONS BY CLINT HANSEN

ZONDERVAN®

Stories Behind the Great Traditions of Christmas
Copyright © 2003 by Andrew Collins

Requests for information should be addressed to:
Zondervan, *3900 Sparks Dr., SE, Grand Rapids, MI 49546*

ISBN 978-0-310-63160-6 (custom)

Library of Congress Cataloging-in-Publication Data

Collins, Ace.
    Stories behind the great traditions of Christmas / Ace Collins; illustrations by
Clint Hansen. – 1st ed.
        p. cm.
    Includes index.
    ISBN 0-310-24880-9
    1. Christmas. 2. Christmas decorations. I. Title.
GT4985.C5475 2003
394.2663—dc21   2003010892

Any Internet addresses (websites, blogs, etc.) and telephone numbers in this book are offered as a resource. They are not intended in any way to be or imply an endorsement by Zondervan, nor does Zondervan vouch for the content of these sites and numbers for the life of this book.

Cover design: Kristen Ingebretson
Interior illustration: Clint Hansen
Interior design: Emily Ghattas

Original package design © HarperCollins Christian Publishing
Photo Credits: Shutterstock
Printed in the United States of America

18 19 20 21 22 /LSC/ 22 21 20 19 18 17 16 15 14 13 12 11 10 9 8 7 6 5 4 3 2 1

To the staff and donors
of World Missionary Evangelism,
who, for the past four decades,
have made every day seem like Christmas
for tens of thousands of third-world orphans.
My humble thanks to you
for this great Christian tradition of selfless service.

Special thanks to
Rheda Jones,
Kathy Collins,
John Hillman,
and the Baylor University Library.

CONTENTS

CONTENTS

INTRODUCTION

Before You Wish for an "Old-Fashioned" Christmas. . . .

"It's the most wonderful time of the year," or so the famous Christmas song goes. But for many Americans, a modern Christmas does not seem to hold the spirit, the charm, and the warmth of an old-fashioned holiday. Yet before we bemoan the demise of what we think Christmas was like in the "old days," a time when it wasn't the most commercialized holiday in America, we might want to reexamine what Christmas past really was. There is no doubt that today this holy time of year is our most frenetic, stressful season. It is therefore only natural that Christians lament that the real reason for the season seems to have been largely forgotten in the midst of cookie baking, decorating, and office parties. It seems that the most awesome event in human history, the coming of God to earth as a babe in a manger, has been forever obscured by Santa, shopping, and merrymaking. So is it really "the most wonderful time of the year"?

Before we brood and protest too much over the ruin of what we think Christmas must have been like in generations long past, we might actually feel encouraged about the season we celebrate today when we consider what Christmas was really like in the days of old.

Only in relatively recent times, the past two hundred years, has Christmas even been celebrated by most Christians. Up until the 1800s, the day recognized as Christ's birthday was largely a pagan celebration. Those who bemoan the lack of religious zeal in modern Christmases would have been appalled at the way people in early America celebrated the day. For a majority of people who embraced Christmas throughout history, Christ wasn't a part of the day at all. In most of the world, especially in England and America, Christmas was not a time of worship, prayer, and reflection; rather, it was a day set aside to sing bawdy songs, drink rum, and riot in the streets.

For centuries, Christmas was anything but a holy day. It was most often a sinful parade of excess, a day set aside for ignoring laws and even terrorizing citizens. Mummers, the British carolers of the day, were musicians and actors who roamed the streets, presenting plays and singing songs. Mirroring the boisterous nature of the English Christmas, these songs rarely acknowledged the Christian aspects of the holiday. Those who attended church did so in wild costumes, the messages of many priests were anything but scriptural, and gambling was common during the services. After church the poor often stormed the homes of the elite in mob-like fashion, pounding on doors and windows, demanding the finest food and drink. If the hosts did not respond, the guests broke into the homes and took what they wanted. This combination "holiday" of Mardi Gras and Halloween was nothing like today's Christmas. The drunken celebrations hearkened back to the time when Romans and Greeks marked the winter solstice with a weeklong festival of self-indulgence. As nothing about these celebrations was staid or reverent, many devoted Christians loathed the holiday and considered it an instrument of sin and evil.

How did the Christmas that Christians recognize today as Christ's birthday deteriorate into such an orgy of irreverent excess? For one thing, history tells us that it took over three hundred years for the church to decide on a day on which to honor Christ's birth. In the minds of millions who go to church now, December 25th is the actual day when Mary gave birth to Jesus. It is ironic that an "undeniable" fact many Christians think they know about their faith has no factual basis at all.

The one biblical passage that alludes to the specific time of the incarnation all but rules out winter as being the season of Jesus' birth. Logic clearly dictates that shepherds would not have been out with their flocks during the coldest time of the year. Most modern Bible scholars believe that Christ was probably born in the spring, based on what we now know of Roman census practices. Though they concede that Jesus could have been born in the summer or fall, one fact seems clear: the date of the Savior's birth was nowhere near December 25th. So why do we celebrate Christmas at a time when the birth of Christ could not have taken place? Probably because early church leaders wanted a holy day to counteract the ancient wild festivals held annually around the time of the winter solstice.

Long before the birth of Christ, almost every culture set aside the shortest days of the year as a celebration of the "rebirth" of the sun. For peoples whose livelihood depended on sunlight, the time when the shortest day of the year passed and the days of light became longer was an event to be marked and treasured. It was wonderful to know that the dark days of winter were finally over and spring was just ahead.

As far back as history is recorded, midwinter festivals were held in Babylon and Egypt. The ancient Germans held fertility festivals in midwinter as well. In Phrygia the birth of the sun god Attis was celebrated on December 25th, as was the birth of the sun god Mithras in Persia. The Greeks partied in late December because of the return of the sun, and during this time the Romans celebrated Saturnalia, a festival dedicated to Saturn, the god of peace and plenty. Saturnalia was the party to end all parties, running annually from the 17th to 24th of December. During this festival, public gathering places were decorated with flowers and banners; gifts and candles were exchanged; and the whole population, slaves and masters alike, celebrated with wild abandon.

To avoid religious persecution during this Roman pagan

festival, early Christians decked their homes with Saturnalia holly. Yet for many who had only recently come to know Christ as Lord and Savior, the lure of the party was simply too great. While not actually worshiping Saturn, a majority of Roman Christians still participated in every facet of the weeklong revelry. Church leaders were often horrified as their members fell prey to their old habits and customs. To the leaders it seemed like sin was the central theme of the festival. They knew something had to be done, but what? For years the question remained unanswered.

As the number of Christians increased and the followers of Jesus developed new customs, it would have been natural for them to mark the birth of Christ. Yet ironically, this time of great joy was overlooked. In fact, the early church did not celebrate the birth of Christ at all until 125, when Telesphorus, the second bishop of Rome, declared that church services should be held to memorialize "the Nativity of our Lord and Savior." Still, no day was set aside as the official birth date of Christ. Since no one was quite sure in which month Christ had been born, the first Christmas services were usually held in September, during the Jewish Feast of Trumpets (modern-day Rosh Hashanah). Within a few years, more than a dozen different days had been assigned by various congregations as the birth date of Christ. Eventually, the most common date for celebrating Christ's birth was January 6th, the modern-day religious holiday of Epiphany. The fact that church leaders did not choose to designate a single date for Christmas indicated how little emphasis was placed on this celebration.

By the fourth century, the Roman Empire finally began to convert to Christianity. When this happened, Easter became one of the most celebrated holidays in the realm. Yet as many in the empire came to worship Jesus, the old traditions and holidays continued. So while the persecution may have stopped and Christian faith might have replaced the old pagan ways in much of the empire, the party of Saturnalia, as well as a host of other winter solstice celebrations, flourished. In 274, when the solstice fell on the 25th of December, the Roman emperor Aurelian proclaimed the date as *Natalis Solis Invicti*, the festival of the birth of the invincible sun. This act was more than most Christian leaders of the time could stomach, yet they felt powerless to do anything about it. After all, while many in Rome were Christians, the emperor was not.

In 320 Pope Julius I had grown tired of seeing the birth of Christ celebrated on scores of different days by churches all across the empire. Though he had no particular reason for choosing it, the pope specified December 25th as the official date of the birth of Jesus Christ. This proclamation was in large part ignored, as Christmas still took a back seat to *Natalis Solis Invicti*.

Five years later Constantine the Great, who had recently converted to the Christian faith, introduced Christmas as an immovable feast on December 25th. He also adopted Sunday as a holy day in a new seven-day week. These decisions were no doubt a result of church leaders' lobbying the Roman emperor for a Christian holiday that would cancel out the pagan midwinter celebration. With the power of the government behind this date, they assumed that Saturn and all the partying that went with the marking of this pagan god's day could be forgotten forever.

Their assumption was quickly proven erroneous. Change did not come quickly. With the birth of Christ going head-to-head against the pagan celebrations, many chose to celebrate the pagan holiday and repent after the parties were finished. Some Christians who did choose to mark Christ's birth did so in the same fashion that pagans honored Saturn and other gods, with wild carousing and sinful behavior. Needless to say, the church was not pleased. Things became so bad that the way Christmas was celebrated even became one of the planks that helped overthrow the English monarchy in 1649.

Oliver Cromwell was a politician who came from an obscure background, rose up in the ranks of Parliament, and led a rebellion that overthrew King Charles I. As a member of the Puritan sect, the most conservative Protestant movement of the era, and as Britain's new "Lord Protector," Cromwell set about trying to restore order and create a democracy. During his fifteen years of rule, the British Empire would change dramatically in a host of different ways. Yet for the common people, the most profound proclamation that came from Cromwell's reign might have been his banning of all Christmas festivities. Much to the horror of the majority of the nation's citizens, Cromwell outlawed Christmas celebrations. Those who took to the streets for merrymaking, singing of carols, or participating in any of the old traditions of the day would be arrested, fined, jailed.

Cromwell, like many others who headed the Catholic and Protestant movements of the time, believed that Christmas should be a sober day of reflection. Unless it fell on a Sunday, it should be treated no differently than any other day of the week. People should go about their daily activities, do their work, and go home to quietly consider what Christ meant in their lives. No gifts should be given, no toasts made, and no carols sung. It was to be a solemn, colorless day.

For his entire rule, Cromwell managed to put a cap on the traditionally riotous English Christmas behavior. Yet after he died and was replaced by his son, the commoners demanded the restoration of the old-fashioned Christmas celebrations. When Richard Cromwell, Oliver's son and England's new leader, refused, the door was opened for a rebellion. With the promise of making Christmas what it had been, Charles II was welcomed back to the throne, and the Puritans were tossed out in the streets.

Charles, and those who followed him, restored the debauchery of Christmas past. Many in the royal family even encouraged the social chaos and misbehavior by contributing liquor and food for the celebrations. A popular song of the time was a tribute to the return of Charles and the restoration of the Christmases of old.

Now thanks to God for Charles' return,
Whose absence made old Christmas mourn,
For then we scarcely did it know,
Whether it Christmas were or no.

With the holiday again a drunken street celebration, songs of the era, including "We Wish You a Merry Christmas," alluded to the nature of the carnival. Large bands of men would go to upper-class homes demanding food, drink, and money. If the homeowners did not comply, their houses were often looted. When the old carol mentions the singers want pudding, an underlying threat can been heard in the line, "We won't leave until we get some." Those who lived in the palatial homes the crowds visited knew the rioters would not depart until they had gotten what they wanted. So even though the royal class had returned to power, many of them feared Christmas as a day of unpredictable violence.

Church leaders of all denominations were aghast at the return of the pagan Christmas celebrations, but they were also powerless to do anything about it. In fact, except for the Church of England and the Catholic Church, churches simply closed their doors and ignored Christmas altogether. The police usually wrote off the often violent day as a tradition, so few lawbreakers were arrested. For generations, in many areas of London, Christmas was a day when women and children feared to venture into the streets.

Over the next two centuries the hope for a Christ-filled

Christmas might have been lost altogether if it had not been for many Catholic and Anglican churches stubbornly holding Christmas Eve and Christmas Day services. Other than these gatherings of worship and the quiet reflections of some families that shared the story of the Savior's birth at home, Christmas was anything but holy in almost all of the English-speaking world.

After failing to stop the sinful nature of Christmas celebrations in England, the Puritans attempted to simply outlaw Christmas in the New World. Beginning with the landing of Englishmen at Plymouth Rock in 1620, the holiday was banned throughout New England. Churches did not meet on this day, and businesses were ordered to stay open. Anyone who was caught celebrating Christmas in any way was subject to arrest and fines. These laws remained in effect for more than 150 years, through the Revolutionary War. Christmas was so largely ignored in early America that beginning in 1789, and on each Christmas for the next sixty-seven years, Congress met on December 25th. During these meetings, no one stopped to acknowledge Jesus' birth.

In spite of the early success at outlawing Christmas in the New World, boatloads of immigrants soon overpowered the wishes of the Puritans. The anti-Christmas laws may have remained on the books, but they were soon ignored. In most American cities, the "Lords of Disorder" took over the streets on December 25th. The drunken parties and gang riots grew so bad that in 1828 the New York City Council met in special session to discuss the issue, and a special police force was formed just to deal with the unlawful conduct of citizens on Christmas Day. Yet even as New York put men in uniform out in the streets to protect life and property from the unruly Christmas revelers, the spirit of the season was about to change.

While in England and America Christmas had become little more than an excuse to party, in Germany the holiday had evolved into a time when family and friends gathered to share food and fellowship and to acknowledge and celebrate the birth of the Savior. In homes throughout Germany, Christmas was the second most holy day of the year, eclipsed only by Easter. This day was especially important to children. The music, the simple decorations, the homemade treats, and the evergreen trees that could be found in many homes made Christmas the most anticipated time of the year.

When Queen Victoria married her cousin, Germany's Prince Albert, in 1840, the English Christmas was transformed as well. Albert brought with him the reverent and family-oriented German traditions of the season, which turned Christmas celebrations in Windsor Castle into a family affair. Soon British families picked up on the way the royals were spending their Christmas and adopted the new traditions. For the first time, peace on earth seemed like it might have a chance on December 25th in the British Isles. Yet it took a combination of several elements to make Christmas a universally accepted time of joy and family gatherings.

In America on Christmas Eve 1822, a minister and educator, Clement Clarke Moore, shared a poem he'd written with his children. "A Visit from St. Nicholas," now known as "The Night Before Christmas," would soon do more than entertain Moore's small New York family. Printed the next year in the New York Sentinel, the poem about the jolly old elf would dramatically change the way Americans looked at the season. For the first time, children were seen as an important part of Christmas. The door was now open for the holiday to be reshaped into one that children of all ages could view as their own.

Then, in 1834, when Charles Dickens's *A Christmas Carol* was published, another step was made in stressing the meaning and importance of Christmas. At the heart of Dickens's story were charity, hope, love, and family. This book was written at a time when the Industrial Age had created a culture in which money and hard labor seemed to rule every facet of society. Holidays had been all but eliminated. Men worked twelve hours a day, six days a week. Children were often put to work in factories at the age of eight or nine. No one had time to stop for even a moment to examine the wonder of life, much less reflect on the birth of a Savior. With Scrooge representing the common thinking of almost all industrialists of the time in both England and the United States, *A Christmas Carol* made people take a second look at their values.

Over the next twenty to thirty years, Christmas evolved from a holiday characterized by drinking and riots into a day of family, giving, and worship. Thanks to Moore's St. Nick,

Santa Claus was everywhere—in stores, on street corners, and in advertising displays. Buying presents and decorating trees became important. In America, states began to declare Christmas an official holiday. Finally, after eighteen centuries of all but ignoring the day, churches began to open their doors for believers to worship, sing songs about Christ's birth, and celebrate not just the death and resurrection of Jesus at Easter, but his incarnation as well. Perhaps ironically, with the introduction of Santa and Scrooge, and with the commercialization of Christmas, those living in America and England finally got a chance to experience the real meaning of Christmas. Santa put an end to the drunken riots and brought peace to the season, and this allowed millions to reflect on the peace offered by the babe's birth in a manger.

The "first Christmas" was a simple time of beauty and wonder. The birth of Christ was less about celebration than it was about family. Though many today may grow tired of the commercialization of Christmas, in reality it has opened the door for Christ to once again become the focal point of the season, and for family, especially children, to be at the heart of the celebration. So today, much more than in the past, we can truly sing, "It's the most wonderful time of the year!"

1

ADVENT

Advent is a word often heard during the weeks leading up to the Christmas season, but as many churches do not actually celebrate Advent, a great number of people do not understand its meaning or its place in church history. To millions, Advent is about wreaths, candles, and calendars. While these three elements are a way to mark the Advent season and have become an essential part of the celebration of this tradition, maybe even overshadowing the four weeks of Advent itself, there is a great deal more to Advent than this.

Advent is a Latin word meaning "the coming." Officially established by church leaders in the sixth century, Advent was originally meant to be a time when Christians reflected on the meaning of Christmas and when new believers spiritually prepared themselves for baptism. Beginning on the Sunday nearest November 30th and running until Christmas Eve, Advent was essentially four weeks set aside to contemplate what the coming of Jesus meant not only to the world but to every individual's soul. Hence, while recognized and organized by the church, Advent was also supposed to be a time of personal retrospection and growth. Today, fourteen hundred years after the first Advent season, many families use the symbols of Advent—wreaths, candles, and calendars—to bring the spiritual meaning of Christmas alive in a way that teaches minds, touches hearts, and reflects the original purpose of the tradition.

To the early Christians, three different meanings were to be found in the days of Advent, or the days of the coming. The first was the coming of the Son of God to earth in human form as the babe in the manger. The second was the coming of Jesus into the lives, hearts, and actions of those who accepted him as their Savior. The third was the future coming when Jesus will return to the earth as a king. As times changed and the world came to view Christmas in terms of the baby Jesus and not the role he played on earth and the role he will play in his future kingdom, the meaning of Advent changed as well.

Until World War II, most people who celebrated Advent dwelled more on the final coming, the time when Jesus would return, than on the first coming, the birth of the child. But as Christmas evolved into a holiday for children, Advent also evolved into a time to remember the child in the manger. A part of the missionary zeal of the holiday may have been lost, but for most people who celebrate Advent, the tenderness and love that was presented in the story of the first Christmas has come to mean even more during the Advent season.

Even in the early church, the clergy and the laypeople

looked for tangible ways to help believers remember the season of Advent. In far northern Europe, the Vikings who had converted to Christianity grasped upon the idea of Advent with an exuberance that did not exist in the rest of world. Because the Norse winters were so long and dark, the light that Jesus brought to the earth, along with the promise of everlasting life beyond the bounds of a harsh world, meant a great deal to these new believers. Out of this faith and their cultural interpretation of the Christmas season, the Vikings created the Advent wreath.

The evergreen tree was a wonderful inspiration to the people of northern Europe. Trapped by long harsh winters, going weeks suffering through black cold nights and short bitter days, these people looked upon the heartiness and strength of the fir trees with awe. During a time when almost everything else died, here was a plant that even winter could not stunt or stop. Because of this, the Christians of this region saw the tree as a symbol for faith. During the season of Advent, they took limbs from the evergreen and shaped them into a wheel-like decoration. Then, to mark the passing days and remember the strength of their faith, they placed a candle on the wreath to represent the light brought to the world with Christ's birth. These Advent wreaths were the first symbols used to mark the monthlong period anticipating Christmas.

Over time the custom of the Advent wreath spread across Europe. As it did, more candles were added, one for each week of the season. Though the candles varied in color from church to church and from country to country, the meaning of each light remained the same. Three of the candles, most commonly purple, represented what many Christians believed to be the most precious gifts of Christmas: hope, peace, and love. The final candle, most often red in color, symbolized the joy of new life gained through the gift of Christ's sacrifice on the cross. Some added a white candle to the wreath. It was lit on Christmas Eve and stood for Jesus' birth.

For centuries, the wreath was the sole symbol of Advent, but during the late Middle Ages, stand-alone candles joined the wreath in marking the importance of the four weeks of worship and reflection. Initially one large candle was used. Marks were made on the candle to represent each day between the first Sunday of Advent and Christmas Eve. In churches and homes, the candles were lit daily and allowed to burn until they reached the next mark. Over the course of a month, the candle would be used up.

Other traditions included using many different candles, one lit during each day of Advent. Some families incorporated prayers into each lighting ritual. On the final day, when all the candles were lit, the wick of a large candle was ignited. Slowly, each of the smaller candles would be extinguished until only the one standing for Christ remained to light the room.

The Advent candles took on special meanings in many churches. One candle was lit during each Sunday of the celebration. Usually the first candle represented the prophets who predicted the coming of Jesus. The second candle represented the Bible and its message. The third candle came to stand for Jesus' mother Mary and her acceptance of her mission. On the final Sunday of Advent, a candle was lit for John the Baptist, the man who told the world that a Savior would be coming soon. Most churches that participated in this practice had a larger candle that stood in the middle of the other four. This candle was lit on Christmas Day and stood for Jesus.

The Advent tradition that is most common today is also the newest—the advent calendar. The Advent calendar originated in Germany a century and a half ago. This children's favorite has probably done more to keep alive the ancient tradition of marking the weeks leading up to Christmas than any other custom or tradition.

Since Germans celebrated Christmas as a children's holiday well before the rest of the world caught onto the concept, it is not surprising that these people adapted the marking of the days of Advent into a ritual that children would find fascinating. Two centuries ago, in many German homes an Advent wreath was hung, but instead of candles, twenty-four tiny bags were placed in the wreath. Beginning on December 1, each day the children opened a new bag, inside of which was a special treat. For eager children, it was like getting a gift every day.

The Advent calendar was an outgrowth of these treat-wreaths and the old custom of using a chalk line to mark off the days from December 1 until Christmas. As a majority of people could not read during the 1800s, and even fewer had access to a calendar, many families would make a mark on their door on the first day of December. Then they would continue to add marks until the marks totaled twenty-five. This is how they knew when to celebrate the birth of Christ.

Gerhard Lang's mother took the concept of marking the days a step further. Using a large prenumbered board, she hung twenty-four pieces of candy with string, one by the number for each day of the month. Gerhard was allowed to take down one treat per day during the first twenty-four days of December. When the candy was gone, Christmas had arrived.

By the turn of the nineteenth century, Lang had grown into a man and was a partner in the printing firm Reichhold and Lang. Remembering how his mother had counted down the days until Christmas, he printed and sold twenty-four tiny pictures that could be glued to any large calendar. The concept quickly became popular, and by 1908 Lang was producing calendars that had doors or windows that could be opened. Inside each door was the drawing of a piece of candy, a toy, or a Christmas decoration. Overnight, the "Munich Christmas Calendar" became one of the most popular Christmas traditions in Germany. By the end of World War II, the custom had spread across Europe and to the United States. By this time the calendars' windows not only hid children's presents but some also opened to Bible verses and pictures from the nativity scene. Such calendars were for sale in stores and catalogs in almost every corner of the world.

Today Advent calendars are one of the most common ways to count down the days before Christmas. Colorful and inexpensive, some secular, others filled with spiritual images, the imagery presented on each new calendar helps stir excitement about the coming of Christmas. And even though few who use the calendars realize it, that anticipation of "the coming" is what Advent is really all about.

In worship services, wreaths, candles, or calendars, Advent is much like a movie preview. Each of its forms and symbols marks the time leading to the special event that is about to take place. Advent heightens the senses and emotions and sets the stage for the wonder of Christmas. When presented in the proper way, the way in which the early church intended, Advent also plants the spiritual seeds that grow into an understanding of the reason for this special season. Christmas is still Christmas without Advent, but the festive four-week countdown puts the holiday into the proper perspective.

~ 2 ~
ANGELS

Even in forums that ignore Jesus' tie to the Christmas holiday, angels often find a prominent place. For reasons few can explain, throughout history these heavenly creatures have touched hearts and changed minds, they have caused people to reflect and reconsider, and they have represented the force of good in such profound ways that even evil seems to bow down before them. And while it is written that they are with us always, perhaps it is during Christmas that they seem most real to us.

During the holiday season, angels seem to be in as many places as Santa. Angels fly through the season as often as snowflakes, and their wings and halos are front and center in almost every aspect of the numerous Christmas festivals and celebrations. They can be found in music, in television shows, and in all kinds of advertisements. Angels are the stars of movies, the subjects of books, and the fund-raising symbols of numerous organizations. Angels are one of the most popular ornaments and decorations and one of the most familiar designs on wrapping paper. They are used as outdoor decorations, perch atop Christmas trees, and shimmer on festive sweaters.

The dictionary defines an angel as "a divine winged messenger." While accurate, this definition fails to touch on the warm and personal relationship that angels have traditionally had with humankind. Throughout history, angels have been protectors as well as messengers, and while commanding reverence and awe, they have also projected compassion and understanding. Perhaps that is why we call a person who does something wonderful an angel.

Angels are mentioned throughout the Bible. Yet when most people contemplate angels, they think primarily of the Christmas story. There can be little doubt that the many appearances of these heavenly creatures in the early pages of the New Testament served to reinforce the importance of the birth of Christ and the impact his life would have on the world. Yet these appearances also gave angels personalities and human qualities that allowed people to strongly identify with them. While angels have always been mysterious and sometimes frightening, as bearers of good news they have been welcomed.

The Gospel of Luke tells us that an angel named Gabriel visited Mary and assured her that she was part of God's greatest plan for humankind. An angel visited Joseph as well. Angels also announced "good tidings of great joy" to shepherds in nearby fields the day Christ was born. And in each of these cases, the biblical writers give us the sense that angels were not just announcing incredible news; they were carefully watching over and protecting each participant in this great drama.

The importance of angels can best be seen by the space they were given in the Gospels. Not one of the biblical scribes described the shepherds or the wise men or went into detail concerning their conversations with Mary and Joseph. None of the writers painted a descriptive picture of the manger or even bothered to identify the time of year when Jesus was born. But in both accounts of the birth of Jesus found in the New Testament, several verses are devoted to what the angels said and how they appeared. In the accounts found in Matthew and Luke, it is obvious that even the earliest Christians were drawn to these wondrous figures and knew full well their importance and power.

Many children grow up being taught that angels are always watching out for them. More than likely, this belief is based on the actions of the angels during that first Christmas. The angels were portrayed as beings of grace, beauty, compassion, knowledge, and power—who wouldn't want someone like that on their side? And since that time two thousands years ago, millions have longingly looked to the heavens during moments of crisis, hoping that an angel would come to guide them as well.

The image of angels as watchkeepers had to have been very important to the early Christians. As these people were living in times when persecution or death could come at any moment, knowing that the angels who would one day trumpet

Christ's return were watching out for them had to be a great comfort. That is probably why angels are seen in so many works of art created by Christian artists during the first few hundred years of church history.

When Christmas worship services were first held in the fourth century, there can be no doubt that angels were mentioned. And when the missionaries took the gospel throughout Europe in the Dark Ages, the stories of angels accompanied them. The impact of the angels in these missionaries' work is clearly evident in the straw Christmas angels that were crafted by converted Vikings in Scandinavia. These Norse people were some of most feared warriors in the world, yet when they accepted Christ and celebrated Christmas, the first holiday ornaments they created were angels.

In the Middle Ages, carvings, paintings, and sculptures of angels could be found in every nation in Europe. They had become so central to many Christians' faith that in some countries' traditions an angel, usually in the form of a small girl, helped St. Nicholas deliver Christmas presents.

During the Renaissance, the master artists painted angels in many works dealing with Christ's life. Yet the most common setting for paintings of angels seemed to be in scenes set in Bethlehem. These winged subjects were almost always portrayed as powerful, imposing, yet gentle beings. These Renaissance paintings, which were so important to the reawakening of the world after the Dark Ages, presented images of angels that kept them alive in people's hearts and minds. In that sense, the artists brought angels out of myth and legend and placed them as living creatures in the real world.

In Germany, when homemade ornaments began to appear on Christmas trees, the first ornaments most children created were angels. This practice continued through the Middle Ages, and when England and America finally began to celebrate Christmas as a family holiday in the mid-1800s, some of the first commercial ornaments displayed in stores were angels.

As the Christian faith took root in South America, children were taught that their nightly prayers were taken to Jesus on the wings of angels. At Christmastime, these same angels delivered all their holiday wishes too.

Christmas carols embraced angels to almost as great an extent as they did Christ. "Angels from the Realms of Glory," "Angels We Have Heard on High," "Hark! The Herald Angels Sing," and scores of other Christmas hymns reflect the admiration and fascination that has bonded Christians to angels for two millennia.

In today's often cynical world, it is ironic that angels seem to be more important than ever. They are the subject of hundreds of books, new songs, documentaries, movies, and even a long-running network television series. In almost every case, the angels presented in historic and fictional works are beautiful creatures who possess the wondrous qualities found in the Bible's telling of the Christmas story.

Hollywood has latched onto angels time and again. It has portrayed them in numerous ways, from very serious to extremely funny. Yet when angels are coupled with Christmas, the message becomes clear: angels are creatures who touch our hearts and bring reason and peace to a universe that is often filled with hopelessness and chaos.

In the movie *Penny Serenade*, a child playing an angel foreshadows the child's death. But in part because of that Christmas-pageant angel, the family finds hope again. And in the incredibly moving *It's a Wonderful Life*, the lead character realizes the difference he had made in the world only when a gentle angel guides him through a journey of discovery. In these two motion pictures, as well as in scores of others produced in secular Hollywood, angels are presented not as fantasy creatures but as living facets of the Christmas season.

Why are angels such an important part of Christmas? Probably because without them, there would have been nothing to herald the coming of Christ onto the human stage. It was the angels who explained what was happening to Joseph, Mary, and the shepherds. How would they have known what to do or where to go if these heavenly beings had not served as their guides? Hence, the angels were a part of God's plan from the beginning and were essential to the final equation. They ushered Jesus to earth, and they announced his ascension back to heaven. Throughout the Bible they are depicted as holy, wise, and mighty spirits that communicate and obey the will of God, minister to his people, and glorify him in all his majesty.

During the days when the story of the birth of Jesus is brought to life through song, Scripture, and nativity scenes, we are reminded that the angels were there for those at the first Christmas and are still there for us today. And unlike Santa, angels are not fictional creations but a living part of life and faith.

~ 3 ~

BIRTHDAY CAKE FOR JESUS

The tradition of baking birthday cakes has existed as long as recipes for cakes have been distributed and calendars have recorded the days, weeks, and years. It is a well-established fact that throughout most of the world, marking the passing of another year of life remains one of the most important traditions for people of every race and culture. Therefore, it seems only natural that a Christmas tradition of baking a cake to recognize the birth of Jesus would have developed as well.

Though there are no written records to indicate where or when baking a birthday cake for Jesus originated, it is likely that this tradition dates back only a few hundred years. Though a few sources claim these sweet treats were first served in England, it is more than likely that this holiday tradition started in Germany, where Christ's birth was celebrated in a more overtly religious fashion from the Middle Ages on.

To bring special meaning to the holidays, the Germans embraced symbolism, such as the Christmas tree and the use of nativity scenes, in their annual holiday traditions. Catholics and Protestants alike attended Christmas Eve services in their churches. Children especially looked forward to Christmas because they would get to sing songs, receive presents, and eat special treats served only during the holidays. As food was an important part of family gatherings in Germany, as was passing along beliefs from one generation to the next, traditions and historical lore meant a great deal to the people of this area. So it was a natural evolution to include a birthday cake for Jesus as part of a family Christmas celebration.

For believers who lived during this period, the baking of the cake accomplished several important functions. First of all it gave children something to look forward to with great anticipation. Cake, like most sweets, was a rare treat; therefore, getting to enjoy cake meant something special was taking place. This atmosphere and the attitudes it created naturally opened the door to the retelling of the story of the Incarnation. It also gave parents a chance to explain why Jesus' birth and life were still important.

The little ancient information that can be found concerning the Christmas birthday cakes of the past indicates that they were often baked with special treats inside. Marbles, small metal animals, or coins were dropped into the batter. Then, after the children had heard the story of Jesus' birth, said a prayer, and the pieces were cut, the real fun began. Kids anxiously and carefully cut into their slice of cake to find what treasures were hidden inside.

The cakes were usually white, representing the purity of Jesus. If any icing was applied, it was often red, signifying the blood that the baby grown into a man would eventually shed for sinners. The fact that the cake rose as it was baked represented the resurrection of Christ. The single candle that usually topped the cake was symbolic of the light Christ brought to the world and the fact that that light would never be extinguished. In some cases, the light also represented the star that the wise men followed to Jesus' hay crib. Finally, the cake's sweet taste was used to explain the wonderful life that awaited anyone who became a Christian.

In the 1800s, after England and America began to celebrate what is now considered a traditional family Christmas, the baking of the birthday cake for baby Jesus became more common in these two countries. While this tradition was never as widely practiced as gifts, trees, and Santa Claus, it did not die out. In many homes the baking of the cake was the highlight of the season.

In the past twenty years or so, thanks in part to churches and Christian schools reviving the old custom, baking a birthday cake for Jesus has become a rapidly growing tradition. Recipes can be found in new holiday cookbooks and on the internet. There are also instructions that spell out what each of the cake's ingredients symbolize and how best to bring this custom into a family's holiday celebration. Though there is some variance in the lessons taught from church to church and home to home, in most cases the symbolism that exists today is very close to that first taught by Germans more than five hundred years ago.

Why is the baking of a birthday cake for Jesus just now beginning to come out of the shadows and into the mainstream of Christmas traditions? Probably for the same reasons that led to the initiation of the practice. Having children come together with their parents or grandparents to bake a cake for Jesus' birthday offers a way to distinguish the reason for the season from the commercial aspects that are found in almost every facet of a modern Christmas. It gives adults the chance to fully explain the real reason that the holiday exists. The fact that meaningful family conversations have traditionally taken place in the kitchen while a meal is being prepared sets the table for this experience being one that is comfortable, fun, and informative. Thus, the most elemental meanings of Christ's birth and life can be explained while mixing the ingredients, stirring the batter, and decorating the cooked cake. Yet perhaps most important is the final element of the tradition that might make the most lasting impression. Singing the "Happy Birthday" song to Jesus brings the baby in the manger to life and clearly places Christ at the center of the annual holiday season.

Just as Jesus and his family were together on the day of his birth, a family coming together to bake a cake reminds them that each Christmas is an important time. At Christmas children, grandparents, mothers, fathers, aunts, uncles, and cousins unite and rejoice in the blessings that they have been given over the year. They share gifts and stories and get to know each other in new ways while remembering the holidays of the past. When partaking of a piece of Jesus' birthday cake, the real meaning of Christmas renews and reawakens the importance of sharing the love that was brought to earth through the birth of the Savior. This tradition also reinforces how that love creates a special bond within the family itself. Hence, a simple birthday cake brings history's most wonderful birthday party into focus and shines special light at the family table during each holiday season.

~4~

BOXING DAY

In almost every English-speaking nation in the world, except the United States, Boxing Day is one of the Christmas holiday's most honored traditions. Yet even though most Americans don't know anything about this unique custom, a great number of U.S. charities benefit from the spirit generated by the celebration of Boxing Day in England.

The origin of Boxing Day probably goes back eight centuries, to the Middle Ages. In both large and small churches throughout England, money boxes were placed near the buildings' entrances. These metal boxes, first brought to the British Isles by Roman soldiers as containers used to keep winnings from games of chance, found their way into sanctuaries as a means of gathering special offerings tied to the Feast of St. Stephen. Held each year on December 26th, this feast honors the early apostle who was stoned for his belief in Christ and for preaching the gospel. In his final words Stephen had urged God not to punish his killers, thus emulating the standard of forgiveness that Christ taught and that all Christians are supposed to embrace. It was obvious that Stephen was a man with a huge heart and a tremendous giving spirit; the church wanted its members to imitate these qualities.

Some legends state that the tin boxes used by Roman soldiers in gambling were first brought into churches because Roman soldiers had gambled for Christ's clothing as he died on the cross. These boxes therefore became symbols representing the gift of Christ's sacrifice. This legend might have some basis in fact, but it is more likely that the boxes were used in churches because they were plentiful, durable, and cheap. In memory of St. Stephen, church members were asked to place special offerings in the "alms" box throughout the year to help the area's needy families. The box was kept locked until the Feast of St. Stephen, when it was opened by the priest and the contents were distributed to the poorest of the poor.

Though not really associated with Christmas, this version of Boxing Day's origin fits well with the spirit of voluntary giving that is supposed to accompany the holiday season. While this is the oldest of the legends concerning the birth of this English holiday, it is the only version that does not center on Christmas.

Another theory about the holiday's beginnings is tied to the rowdy English Christmases of the Middle Ages. The wealthy, who were visited on December 25th by mobs of common people demanding food and drink, used servants to hand out the treats, as well as to straighten up the household and the grounds once the rowdy masses departed. As a way of thanking their household workers for performing these extra duties, the elite would give their servants boxes filled with cloth, leather goods, and food. Who got what was determined by the worker's status in the household and the size of his or her family. It is debatable whether or not this custom was the beginning of the boxing holiday, yet it probably did form the roots of another tradition that might have initiated Boxing Day.

Three centuries ago, servants in England began to bring their own boxes to work on the day after Christmas. Probably due to the boxed gifts given to servants in earlier days, it became a tradition that all employers would put coins into the boxes as a special year-end bonus. Leftovers from the Christmas feast were often also placed in the boxes. Within a hundred years, it had become common practice for the wealthy to give monetary bonuses to bakers, blacksmiths, newspaper boys, butchers, and everyone else who provided services for the household.

Boxing Day took on its current form and gained status as a fully recognized holiday during the reign of Queen Victoria. With Victoria and her husband, Prince Albert, leading the way, upper-class households were expected to share gifts with the poor on December 26th of each year, thereby increasing the Christmas generosity of the upper class to those who garnered so much of Christ's attention while he walked on earth: the sick, the lame, the poor, and the forgotten. To underscore its importance to the British people, Boxing Day was even a banking holiday at a time when financial institutions in the rest of the world remained open on Christmas.

Today Boxing Day continues to be celebrated on December 26th in Great Britain, as well as in Canada, Australia, New Zealand, and even parts of China. The focus of the day is much the same as it was when old Roman gambling boxes were opened to share money with the needy. The holiday is about recognizing the mission to reach out to those who are not as fortunate, reaching deep into hearts and pockets to give sincere gifts of charity and love.

While Boxing Day in the United Kingdom has traditionally involved very personal giving, in America a host of different charities have adopted the essence of this British holiday in a more corporate fashion. The first to fully understand the power of the special compassion felt by millions at Christmas was the Salvation Army. For more than a century, this organization's bell ringers have been out in force in the weeks before Christmas, seeking donations to fund its many Christian programs. Over the years scores of other groups have joined them.

Churches have gotten into the act as well. Almost every denomination takes up special collections during the holidays. While many now use envelopes or collection plates, a few still employ tin boxes that resemble the ones opened centuries ago in churches on St. Stephen's Day. Hundreds of thousands of people in the United States also go out in groups at Christmas to make sure that families who have fallen on hard times are given boxes of food, clothing, and toys during the holiday season. So while Boxing Day is all but unknown in America, its spirit is very much alive.

The origin of Boxing Day is not nearly as significant as what the outgrowth of this annual tradition has come to mean to millions of the world's poorest people. Thanks to this wonderful holiday tradition, neighbors have been encouraged to reach out to neighbors in a very personal way. And in the midst of the Christmas season, Christian charity is played out in a fashion that reflects well on the life of the man whose birth we celebrate on December 25th and those, like Stephen, who have followed his example. This is one tradition that needs to be expanded!

5

CANDY CANES

There are probably as many legends centered on the candy cane as on any other Christmas tradition. Many of the tales that are known today about this familiar hook-shaped peppermint stick are probably as much fable as fact. Nevertheless, in the last seventy-five years, the symbolism of the candy cane, born of legend and now brought to life by a unique striping design, has made it one of the best teaching tools of the holiday season.

Hard candy has been around almost as long as people have been yearning for sweets. For over a thousand years, hard candy has been used to reward children who were good. Yet the multicolored candy that is seen on store shelves today did not exist until one hundred years ago. Because of the time it took to add additional colors by hand, in the past hard candy was usually made in a solid color.

When children began to receive special treats on St. Nicholas's Day in the fourth century, hard candy was probably one of the first things enjoyed. Yet because the ingredients for this candy were not easy to obtain, and most peasants did not have enough money to purchase these treats often, the sweet was probably a rare delicacy in most households. The rarity and the popularity of the treat means that the first Christian legend associated with the candy cane is probably based on actual events.

Church history records that in 1670 the choirmaster at Germany's Cologne Cathedral was faced with a problem that still challenges parents, teachers, and choir directors today. In ancient Cologne, as well as in thousands of churches today, the children in the choir often grew restless and noisy during long services. Most authority figures of the time would have handled this situation through punishment, usually with a switch. Yet the choirmaster, who had seen this tactic used time

and again, knew that the punitive practice only worked for short periods of time. Soon the painful lesson had been forgotten and the children were again fidgeting and whispering to one another.

The choirmaster came up with a sweetly brilliant plan. He sought out a local candy maker, and after looking over the treats in his shop, the music leader paused in front of some white sweet sticks. He knew that children liked this treat, and better yet, it took them a long time to consume the sticks. So this candy seemed perfect for what he needed—a way to keep the children quiet when they were not singing.

Yet the choirmaster wondered if the priests and parents would allow him to give the children in his choir candy to eat during a church service. The congregation and clergy would get upset if the children were not quiet, but they would probably also be offended if the kids were eating candy in the sanctuary.

Then inspiration struck! The choirmaster asked the candy maker if he could bend the sticks and make a crook at the top of each one. When the confectioner assured the director that he could, a plan was hatched. The candy would not be just a treat; it would be a teaching tool. The choirmaster decided that the candy's pure white color would represent the sinless life of Christ. The crook would serve as a way for the children to remember the story of the shepherds who came to visit the baby Jesus. The shepherds carried staffs or canes, and with the hook at the top of the stick, the candy now looked like a cane.

Right before the service, the music leader gathered his flock around him and told them the symbolic story of the white candy stick. The congregation and the priests were enamored with the choirmaster's inventive tale and believed the use of biblical truths in the lesson to be indeed inspired. But the ultimate compliment for the choirmaster came when his choir was so busy enjoying their long-lasting treats that they didn't disturb the Christmas Eve service at all. Thus began the simple candy cane's association with the Christian faith.

Within a hundred years, white candy canes were being placed on Christmas trees in Germany. Some may have known the story the choirmaster told his charges in Cologne, but more likely most of those who hung these treats on the tree did so because the hook made it easy to use. The bottom line was that children could not wait for the time to take the tree down, usually on January 6th, the day of Epiphany, so that they could finally eat the decorations.

Another persistent legend surrounding the candy cane is tied to Oliver Cromwell's rule in England, a time when Christmas celebrations were banned by the Puritan leader. It is said that during this short historical period, a dedicated Christian confectioner created a candy cane as a way for Christians to recognize each other on the street. The candy was supposed to be a type of code or signal, like a secret handshake. These canes, decorated with three tiny red stripes (which represented the Father, Son, and Holy Spirit) and another bold, thick red stripe that demonstrated the redemptive power of Christ's blood, were given out to those who professed Christ as their Savior.

Could this legend be true? Possibly, but as the striping would have had to be accomplished by hand and would have taken a long time, it is doubtful that the candy maker could have distributed very many of the canes. Thus, the symbolic practice would have been observed in only a small part of England, possibly one community or village. Also, though Christmas was officially banned, corporate worship was not, so the need for a symbol of this type would have seemed unnecessary.

More than likely, if this legend of the candy maker is true, it probably happened not during Cromwell's reign, but when all religions but the Church of England were officially banned. The candy maker may have been a member of an outlawed Protestant faith or the Catholic Church and used the cane as a teaching tool. So, though largely unsubstantiated, there probably is some truth in this story and the legend survives to this day.

Europeans must have brought the candy cane with them to the United States before the revolution of 1776. But the treat's identification with Christmas didn't take root until Americans began to celebrate Christmas with presents, trees, and family gatherings two decades before the Civil War. It is said that a German-Swedish immigrant, August Imgard, was the first in the United States to use candy canes as ornaments. In 1847 he placed them on the fir tree he had brought into his Wooster, Ohio, home for a holiday decoration. The idea quickly caught on. There are many American Christmas illustrations from the second half of the nineteenth century that show the candy cane as part of holiday festivities, but in each case the candy is solid white.

By the turn of the century, the candy cane was incredibly popular throughout the year, but it didn't take on its current look until the 1920s. Bob McCormick, who ran a small confectionery in Albany, Georgia, found a way to hand-twist colors into the candy canes. Soon the process was being used by others. An Indiana candy maker, whose brother was a priest, knew the old story of the red-and-white candy cane being used as a way to identify Christians in England. A Christian, the Indiana candy maker created canes that reflected this legend, as well as his own belief. Each of this man's festive sticks was made with the symbolism of the Trinity and of the redeeming blood, the hook for the shepherd's staff, and the white for the purity of Christ. It is even said that in this case, the hook was really the upside-down letter J, standing for Jesus. So while the spiritual meaning of the original colored candy cane might well have been a legend in England, within the past century the legendary symbolism has become a reality in the United States and throughout much of the world.

There can be little doubt that hard candy has been associated with the holiday season as long as children have looked forward to seeing St. Nicholas. Yet the candy cane that probably first appeared at a church service in the Middle Ages, used then as a tool to both teach and appease children, has become one of the sweetest reminders of the real reason for the Christmas season and one of the few holiday traditions that portrays the meaning of why Jesus was born.

~ 6 ~

CAROLS AND CAROLING

Caroling, an ancient word referring to dancing or singing songs of praise and happiness, was practiced during all seasons of the year in the Dark Ages, and carols embraced a wide range of subjects. When a fourth-century pope designated December 25th as the day to recognize Christ's birth, it was only natural that many of the secular carols were adapted for songs celebrating the birth of Jesus. The leaders of the church frowned upon this use of pagan music for songs with Christian messages. So the first carols were quickly quashed by the Catholic Church. In fact, as long as the organized church—both Catholic and Anglican—controlled Christmas music, which would be for almost eighteen hundred years, most Christians could not get very excited about carols. It was only when this musical form was taken over by the common people that it brought forth the joy and wonder that can be found in the carols that are sung today.

History records that in 129 a Roman bishop asked that a carol called "Angel's Hymn" be sung at a Christmas service in Rome. And a year later Pope Telesphorus decreed that all

Christian congregations should sing "Gloria in Excelsis Deo" during services recognizing the birth of Jesus. Were these two songs the very first church-endorsed Christmas carols? Perhaps, but as it would be more than two hundred years before the church would designate December 25th as the official birthday of Christ, it is unlikely that either of these carols was sung at Christmas outside of worship services. Hence, early church members might have been familiar with a few Christmas carols, but they probably didn't gather together and sing them at home or on the streets. Maybe that is the reason there is little mention of Christmas music for the next few centuries.

In 760 Comas, a Christian composer living in Jerusalem, wrote a Christmas hymn for a Greek church service. This song seemed to start a movement toward writing more musical works that dealt with Christ's birth. But because the tunes were rarely melodic, and all of them were written in Latin (which the audiences didn't understand), these carols didn't catch on with the general population. So in the midst of the darkest and coldest days of the year, the harsh and stiff Christmas music of the church offered very little to make the birth of Jesus a time of great joy and celebration for most Christians.

Therefore, music was rarely associated with Christmas during the Dark Ages.

In 1223 St. Francis of Assisi built on a Christmas tradition created by a church leader in tenth-century Rome by constructing a nativity scene outside his church. He invited children not just to view his vision of what the first Christmas looked like but to join him in the midst of the display and sing Christmas songs. Francis taught them songs in their own language rather than in Latin, and when they understood each song's meaning, a new enthusiasm gripped the singers. These children, singing outside on a cold December evening, were probably the first true Christmas carolers.

Francis's "nativity plays" grew more ornate and complex every year. The carols evolved into "canticles," and the drama often resembled a pageant. These presentations and the songs that were sung during them became so popular that they spread throughout Europe. Soon France, Spain, and Germany were adding their own carols to their nativity plays. Something unique was happening, and because it was going on outside the walls of the church, scores of common people felt like they were a part of it. As these new songs became the property of the common people, the songs took on a life and joy rarely found in church music of the period. Often by borrowing existing melodies from popular folk songs, amateur musicians came up with Christmas songs that were so familiar and easy to sing that almost anyone could quickly learn them.

Most church leaders were shocked by these new carols. In the minds of many parish priests, it was bad enough that the framework for the lyrics was sometimes an old drinking tune, but it was even worse when the lyrics were not biblically correct. Attempts were made to ban songs written by anyone other than trained clergy, but most people just ignored the bans and sang these new carols each Christmas in their homes and on the streets with friends.

Soon professional and amateur carolers could be found throughout Europe. Traveling singers, often called minstrels, picked up on the carols. On their travels, they entertained audiences with these carols during the month of December. When the troubadours moved on to the next "tour" stop, the carols stayed behind. Locals learned them and sang them in taverns, on the streets, and in homes. Children began to band together and perform on street corners in an attempt to raise money. Yet even as Christmas music spread and the joy of singing the carols infected thousands, the church remained unconvinced of the songs' worth. Many in the clergy believed that by losing control of Christmas music, they were also losing control of their faith. So the church continued to fight the movement.

In early sixteenth-century Germany, Martin Luther embraced carols, thereby winning over many German Christians to the songs. Luther sang them with his children and encouraged his growing following to come together and sing them as a congregation. He found great joy in the music of the holiday season and believed the passion it brought to those who sang Christmas songs was to be embraced. Thanks in part to Luther's acceptance of carols, the German carols of this period were better written and much more spiritual than most of those in other European countries.

George Frideric Handel was born in Germany in 1685. When he composed the *Messiah* in 1741, it began to change the church's opinion of "modern" Christmas music. And when, in Austria in 1818, a priest named Joseph Mohr and a schoolteacher named Franz Gruber put their talents together to create "Stille Nacht, Heilige Nacht" ("Silent Night"), the church's acceptance of carols began in earnest. "Silent Night" has since become the most recorded song in history. Yet for carols to become a fully accepted Christmas tradition, it would take the royal marriage of England's beloved queen, Victoria, to her cousin, Prince Albert of Germany, in 1840.

Prince Albert loved to sing, and he was a huge fan of Christmas carols. The royal family therefore learned to sing Christmas songs in German and English. The London newspapers reported the royal family's love of holiday music. In an effort to charm the royal family and win favor, many families and church groups came to Windsor Castle to serenade the queen and her family with their favorite carols. Soon these Victorian carolers made their way throughout London, singing their songs to friends and strangers. But unlike the carols of the Middle Ages, the Victorian carols were sincere expressions of faith, joy, and the wonder of the holiday season.

Within a few years Christmas caroling had spread all across

Britain and was taking Europe by storm. This music, once distrusted by the church, was now being embraced by almost every established denomination.

In the United States, first the Methodists and then the Lutherans brought carols into worship services and organized street carolers from within their congregations. By the end of the Civil War, thousands of churches were using carolers to reach those who did not attend church, to minister to the sick and disabled, and to "advertise" the fact that they had a happy and outgoing congregation.

Unlike the raucous and demanding singing gangs of sixteenth-century England, the new breed of carolers sang simply because they wanted to. The fact that they were often welcomed into homes and served cookies or hot cider mattered little if at all to them. They had discovered that music made Christmas come alive. In a sense, singing a song in the open air with a group of carolers also connected each person to the baby in the manger like no sermon ever could. It seemed that much more than anything else the church was doing in the late 1800s, caroling brought goodwill to people throughout the world.

The huge popularity of caroling created a new market for Christmas music. This is probably the reason that some of the best and most loved carols were written in the seventy-five years after the Civil War. American composers led the way, but songs continued to be composed all over the world. These songs even carried the world through wars, when peace on earth seemed impossible. Yet through the voices of Christmas carolers, the message and hope of the season somehow didn't just survive, at times it actually brought peace.

On Christmas Eve in 1870, during the Franco-Prussian War, a French soldier leaped out of his foxhole in the midst of the battle and began singing the carol "O Holy Night." He was soon joined by other Frenchmen, and all gunfire ceased. The Germans answered with a carol of their own, and for one day the battle stopped and men on both sides celebrated Christmas.

In 1914 a Christmas truce was called during World War I. During the special truce, both sides got together, helped bury the dead, exchanged gifts, and sang Christmas carols.

During World War II, as well as during the wars in Korea and Vietnam, organized caroling was one way that troop morale was bolstered during the holidays. The old songs, the ones that men had sung since childhood, brought together more than their voices; it knit together their spirits, hopes, and dreams.

Caroling is not as popular today as it was fifty years ago. This is in a large part due to the nature of the times. People are incredibly busy, life is fast paced, and America and England are more urban than rural. The fact that recorded Christmas music can be heard in every store and on every street corner has probably made hearing Christmas music an almost mundane experience for many people.

Yet caroling still goes on. Groups still bundle up and seek out places to sing the songs about the birth of the Savior. Carolers can be spotted in malls, in front of schools, and outside churches. These musical troubadours are also an important part of many musicals, movies, television productions, and even music videos. In a very real sense, the music that church leaders thought would destroy Christmas has brought the season to life in the most wonderful way. Carols and carolers are the musical fuel that creates so much joy in the world as their songs touch souls more deeply than perhaps any other facet of Christmas worship.

7

CHRISTMAS CARDS

It would be hard to imagine a modern Christmas without Christmas cards, but the Christmas card is a rather recent addition to the holiday traditions. The fact that Christmas cards took so long to arrive on the scene can be traced to their having to wait for an affordable and reliable postal service, as well as for the growth of the middle class and the development of inexpensive four-color printing methods. Even when all of those things were in place, it took an overworked English knight's childhood memory and a celebrated British artist's brush to make this wonderful Christmas tradition a reality.

Sir Henry Cole was a mover and shaker in mid-nineteenth-century England. It seemed he had his hand in just about everything. Cole was an assistant at the public records office, a writer of books on art and architecture, a publisher and editor of children's books, a director of the London Museum, and the founder of the *Journal of Design*. Because of his wealth and position, Cole moved freely in the upper-class circles, was a popular guest at social events, and was friends with the royal couple, Queen Victoria and Prince Albert. Albert was so impressed with Cole's energy and accomplishments that he often said, "When you want steam, you must get Cole!" But with Cole's busy social calendar and the demands brought on by his jobs, his writing, and his publishing business, the one thing Cole had very little of was time.

In December 1843 Cole's mailbox was stuffed daily with holiday letters from his friends and associates. With pressing deadlines from all his business ventures, Cole could not find a spare moment to sit down and respond to any of these greetings. As the stack grew higher and higher, the publisher worried that by not answering his holiday mail, he would cause a host of hurt feelings among his close friends and associates.

One busy day when Cole was working furiously at his desk, he picked up a rigid piece of paper. Studying it, he folded it in such a way that it resembled a small book. Fascinated with the possibilities he saw before him, he opened the thick paper. As he studied the blank pages, he recalled an assignment he had been given as a schoolboy. During grammar school his teacher had given the students the task of drawing a holiday scene as a gift for their parents. He recalled not only what he had created, but also what his fellow students had drawn on what their teacher had called "Christmas pieces." Cole recalled that each finished product had reflected what Christmas meant to each child. Some depicted biblical scenes, others red roses, a few candy, and yet others families at the holiday dinner table. Cole suddenly realized that by combining that long-ago grammar school assignment with this small folded piece of heavy paper, he had the answer to his annual problem of answering holiday greetings. Within a few hours an enthused and energized Cole left his desk to visit with his friend John Calcott Horsley.

Horsley was a painter whose skill Cole admired. The artist was talented, could work quickly, and like most painters of the era, was always in need of money. As the two men met in Horsley's art studio, Cole showed him a new piece of heavy paper, this one folded three times, and explained what he envisioned should go on the paper. Horsley nodded as the publisher spoke. The artist quickly realized that what he created for Cole would soon find its way into the most celebrated homes in England, including that of Queen Victoria herself. So while Horsley immediately knew that this was a very important assignment, he couldn't have guessed that his work would spawn a huge industry.

Cole wanted Horsley to be creative, but that creativity would be initially confined to the publisher's own vision of Christmas. Inside the "card," Cole wanted a painting of a happy family and friends celebrating around the holiday table. On the card's two outside folds, or side panels as he called them, the publisher instructed Horsley to depict themes that would stir compassion. Cole wanted the elite who received his cards to remember that during the winter months there were poor who needed food and clothing and that helping these people should be in everyone's Christmas thoughts and plans.

Horsley quickly drew the small, colorful images that were

needed for the card, and Cole enthusiastically approved them. At Jobbins of London, a well-known English printer, Cole added the words "A Merry Christmas and a Happy New Year to You." As the press went to work printing 1000 cards, neither the artist nor the publisher realized that the painting of the Victorian family gathering would stir up a great deal more controversy than goodwill.

For Cole, having the largest illustration in his card showing a family group raising their glasses in a toast to the season seemed in keeping with the spirit of the holidays. But when the cards arrived at the homes and businesses of Cole's friends and associates, many who received the cards were distressed. Puritans thought the holiday table image and toast encouraged drinking. In their minds this scene was too reminiscent of a time in the not too distant past when Christmas in England was a day of drunken carousing. Yet in spite of a chorus of such objections, overall the cards made a positive impact.

The next year the same images were printed (this time by Summerly's Home Treasury Office) using lithography, a printing process in which the image to be printed is rendered on a flat surface, such as sheet zinc or aluminum, and is treated to retain ink while the nonimage areas are treated to repel ink. The company sold the greeting cards for one shilling each. Every card that was printed was purchased.

Within two years Christmas cards became the way thousands of English families shared Christmas greetings with friends and loved ones. In fact, with the cards and the national mail service so cheap, the British postal department found itself hard pressed to keep up with the new custom. The government had to hire extra workers just to handle the increase in mail during the holiday season.

Within a decade scores of artists and publishers were creating Christmas impressions that were seen by hundreds of thousands of people each year. The tradition quickly spread across the English Channel, and by the mid-1850s the commercial Christmas card was a reality in almost all of Europe.

While Christmas cards were the rage in Europe during the time of the American Civil War, the custom was still obscure in the United States. The unsettling conditions in America had produced divisions so deep that many had little time to even note Christmas and its traditions. But not long after the Civil War ended, when the nation was united and good times had returned for many, a German-born printer would turn Americans on to the custom of sending Christmas cards.

Louis Prang arrived in Roxbury, Massachusetts, a decade before the Civil War. Trained as a lithographer, he eventually settled in Boston, where he began work as a wood engraver. Soon he branched out into color printing and publishing. After the Civil War, Prang began printing vivid reproductions of some of the world's most famous works of art.

Always searching for ways to impact others with his passions, Prang began to write art books, including *Prang Method of Art Instruction*, *Prang Standards of Color*, and *Prang's Natural History Series*. In 1877 Prang's Aids for Objective Teaching quickly became one of the most popular art texts in the United States. Using this book as a springboard, he organized the Prang Educational Company and published the industry standard for drawing books that were used by art schools. Yet as profound as Prang's impact was on the American educational system, he would gain his greatest fame by producing America's first mass-distributed Christmas cards.

Though Prang had been printing Christmas cards for himself and a few friends since 1856, he didn't fully comprehend the potential of the holiday greeting card until he attended the Vienna Exposition, a gathering of businesses involved in the printing industry, in 1873. In an effort to gain clients and win contracts, Prang distributed beautiful four-color business cards. Upon seeing his card, an English woman asked the printer if he had ever thought of using his colorful designs for Christmas cards. Doing some research, Prang discovered that the market for such cards in England was huge. Going back to Boston, he designed and produced his first commercial Christmas cards, exporting all of them to stores in and around London. Because of the rich colors, the American cards were a huge hit.

The next year Prang printed new, even more colorful cards. This time he not only shipped them to England but, using the contacts he had made through publishing art books, sold them in stores throughout northeastern America. Within two years the Prang cards had a corner on the holiday card market in the United States.

By 1880, demand for Prang's Christmas cards had surpassed his abilities as an artist. He needed new ideas. Using newspapers and magazines, the publisher promoted a contest in which people could submit holiday art to Prang Publishing. Those whose art was deemed the best would not only find their works on the next year's cards but would also share $3000 in prize money. The contest was a monumental success, drawing hundreds of entries. In the first year a host of new artists was discovered, and the frenzy that Prang created in searching for new illustrations paved the way for the popularity of Christmas cards in the United States to rival that in England.

By 1890 European printers, using cheaper labor and less expensive printing processes, drove Prang out of the Christmas card business. But as the man who introduced Christmas cards to America and opened up the marketplace to this new custom, the native German will always be remembered as the "Father of the American Christmas Card."

While Prang's Christmas images were rich and beautiful,

they broke no new ground in terms of the themes and images they depicted: families, robins, street scenes. Thomas Nast, the famed illustrator for *Harper's Weekly*, would be the one to add a real New World touch to Christmas cards. It was Nast who, in 1862, created the look of Santa Claus when he drew the art for a printing of Clement Clarke Moore's poem "The Night Before Christmas." Over the years, as Nast continued to add drawings of Santa to his Christmas illustrations, he produced images of the jolly elf in the American countryside, visiting rooftops in cities, and even mingling with soldiers during the Civil War. These unique impressions, at the time found only in America, began to emerge on Christmas cards, while also influencing other artists and printers to produce similar works. By the turn of the century, thanks in no small part to Nast, Santa was a fixture on a large portion of Christmas cards sold in the United States.

It wasn't until the twentieth century that card printers began to produce religious imagery that drove home the real meaning of Christmas. Images of angels, shepherds, and the nativity scene, as well as snow-covered churches, children in prayer, and carolers singing hymns, began to appear on Christmas cards. This "rediscovery" of a biblical Christmas occurred when American and English churches finally began to fling open their doors and embrace Christmas as a time for joy and celebration. Hence, Christmas cards became not only a tool for extending greetings to business associates, friends, and family but also a way to share the gospel with others.

It is doubtful that Sir Henry Cole could have imagined the

incredible popularity of his inspiration. Yet the publisher, who was deeply concerned about the plight of London's poor and forgotten, would have been overjoyed to know that his cards have indeed brought a special joy to the holiday season. He would have loved the fact that many of the cards sold today raise funds for treating children suffering from cancer, for feeding starving masses in third-world nations, for research to end diseases that have plagued humankind for centuries, and for many other worthy causes. Therefore, while the card industry is one of the most commercial of all the holiday businesses, for millions of people the spirit of Cole's first set of cards continues to be realized each year.

Cheap to produce, inexpensive to mail, a holiday tradition that can be embraced by both rich and poor, Christmas cards bring wonder and joy to hundreds of millions of people each year. Though the verses and the images are as varied as those who send them, the ultimate message is that someone cares enough to take the time to send a greeting. For many, this knowledge makes Christmas a great deal brighter.

8

CHRISTMAS SEALS

Today a gift of a halfpenny would seem ridiculous to most people. And so it seemed to people a century ago, when one of the great giving traditions of Christmas was initiated. It began when one person gave a halfpenny to purchase a little stamp for an envelope that was mailed in the month of December. While that stamp would not even provide the cost of the letter's mailing, it would nevertheless begin a movement that would end suffering for millions and make Christmas a time not just of joy and wonder but of hope and healing.

The early days of the twentieth century were not easy ones for children. Throughout Europe and America, millions of kids lived in poverty, and many young people were forced to leave school to work in factories or on farms to help sustain their family's meager existence. But the cruelest blow was that diseases such as polio, scarlet fever, and measles—most of which are now all but extinct—killed hundreds of thousands of children each year.

In Denmark Einar Holboell was more than simply aware

of the world's suffering masses; he saw starving children each day as he walked to work. As a postal clerk, he always knew of families that were living on the edge between life and death. He was also aware of the host of illnesses that senselessly snatched children before they had a chance to really live. These frightful images kept him awake at night and plagued him even in his dreams. Yet of all the diseases, the one that troubled Holboell the most was tuberculosis. Nothing pained him more than watching a child desperately trying to breathe, fearing that each breath was his or her last, and then seeing the family mourn as the inevitable finally happened. TB brutally killed people of every age group, but what it did to a child horrified the postal clerk.

Unlike millions of others around the world who witnessed the effects of tuberculosis firsthand and did nothing, Holboell decided to act. He didn't have the knowledge or education to go into medical research, but he understood that only through science could something be done. What was needed was funding for the research. With his small salary, the clerk didn't have the means to do anything by himself. Yet he would not give up. What ultimately came to him was a plan to create a team of donors who could band together; in the process, this group could save lives and bring great happiness to families who now knew only pain and grief.

As there was always a huge increase in the volume of mail during the Christmas season, creating long hours of extra work, December was generally a time of year that Holboell and those who worked beside him dreaded. Yet in spite of the workload, the clerk loved the holidays because he got to witness firsthand the generous spirits of those who came into the post office. Even in the midst of the coldest winter days, people seemed happier in December. With thoughts of the smiling faces and kind works he witnessed at the post office, an idea came to him.

Going to his boss, Holboell explained his vision for helping those suffering with tuberculosis. He also pointed out that the time to raise money and awareness was during the Christmas season, when people were in the mood to give. Finally, after he had won the supervisor's interest, he unveiled a plan that would allow the post office to raise money to fight TB.

Holboell proposed a very simple fundraiser for the month of December. He suggested that the Danish postal service print a stamplike seal that could be affixed to any mailing envelope. Each seal would cost only a halfpenny, and while the seals would add nothing to each mailing but a bit of color, the clerk figured that if enough people bought them, these seals could help fund treatment and research to fight tuberculosis in Denmark. Holboell's supervisor took the plan to his own boss. The concept rapidly moved through the entire federal post office chain of command. Everyone loved the idea. Even the king of Denmark expressed his approval and provided royal patronage.

The first seal, bearing a picture of the king and queen and the simple words "Merry Christmas," was issued in 1904 and sold in post offices throughout the country. Over four million seals were sold, raising more than $18000. The kindly postal clerk watched in humble awe as the money brought in through his idea funded the construction of two children's hospitals. But as he would find out, this was just the beginning; the next year the sale of Christmas Seals brought even more money to the cause. The fundraiser would continue to grow for years to come.

Across the Atlantic in the United States, generations of Americans had suffered the pain and dread associated with tuberculosis. For most of the 1700 and 1800s, TB was thought of as a death sentence. It was believed that nothing could be done once the illness had invaded the body. In 1873 New York City physician Edward L. Trudeau was diagnosed with TB. Giving up his practice, he moved to upstate New York to await death.

In the peaceful surroundings of the mountains, Dr. Trudeau's condition began to improve. Over time he came to believe that with proper bed rest, good nourishment, fresh air, and lots of sunshine, this monster could be tamed. Armed with that knowledge and a clean bill of health, Trudeau returned to New York City to tell others about his recovery. A decade later, in 1884, he opened the first TB hospital in the United States. On the shores of Saranac Lake, in a one-room building with beds for only two patients, Trudeau became locally famous as the man who could cure TB.

Others soon joined the doctor in providing rest and care for those suffering from tuberculosis. While not all patients were cured, enough shook the illness to provide millions around the country with hope. Yet despite all the testimonies and all the accolades, Trudeau and his army of followers could not raise enough money to build the facilities to treat even 5 percent of those suffering with TB. And even more disconcerting to the medical profession was the fact that the hospitals being built to combat the disease were underfunded, makeshift sanatoriums, some of which did more harm than good.

In 1907 one of the rudimentary TB hospitals was located on the banks of Delaware's Brandywine River. As were most medical facilities of the time, it was in desperate financial condition. The fact that the Brandywine Clinic had a tremendous cure rate did not help its fundraising efforts. As most of its patients were destitute, the sanatorium's future looked as bleak as the future of those suffering with untreated TB. The clinic needed $300 just to keep its doors open through the winter. To Dr. Joseph Wales and the other doctors running the facility, this seemingly small amount might just as well have been a million.

Emily Bissell was a fundraiser for the American Red Cross in Wilmington, Delaware. She knew how to catch people's interest and tap into their compassion. Dr. Wales was well aware of Emily's talents; she was his cousin. Picking up pen and paper, he wrote to Emily about his problem.

"We're down to our last dollar. Unless $300 can be raised somehow, the poor patients will have to be sent home to die. . . . and perhaps to spread the disease to other people. I hope you'll find a way. You've got to help us."

Emily tackled the problem with the same boundless energy she tackled everything else in her life, but this time she hit a wall. It seemed that no one would listen to her pleas. Though Dr. Wales had a great success record with curing TB, even America's rich and wealthy still considered the illness terminal. The same folks who generously gave to the Red Cross told her they were not going to support this hopeless cause. If it had not been for a magazine article, Emily might have been forced to give up, and the Brandywine Clinic might have closed its doors.

Journalist Jacob Riis had watched six of his brothers die of tuberculosis. He knew the horrors of the disease firsthand. Though an American citizen, the writer had been born in Denmark. A family member had written to Riis informing him of the manner in which his native country was fighting TB via a holiday fundraising program known as Christmas Seals. His curiosity aroused, Riis learned all the facts about the program and penned a piece in a northeastern periodical. Few people seemed to note Riis's work; the article prompted little response. If the story had not fallen into Emily Bissell's hands, the Danish fundraising concept might well have been completely overlooked in the United States.

Armed with this novel concept, Emily went back to the drawing board. She sketched a design of a red cross centered in a half-wreath of holly. Above this holiday illustration she wrote the words "Merry Christmas." She then took the idea to the Delaware Red Cross. They approved of the concept but would not donate funds to print the seals. They did, however, lobby and get approval from the national organization for permission to use the red cross as a symbol on the first batch of American Christmas Seals.

Unable to raise the money from any groups, Emily borrowed $40 from friends and obtained an additional commercial loan to print 50,000 seals. Yet as is often the case with enthusiastic people on a mission, she had gotten the cart before the horse. She had not cleared the sale of the seals with the post office. With the seals already printed, the Wilmington postmaster reviewed the idea, listened to the woman's plea, and then told her that the fundraiser would not work. Besides, he noted, as seals were not a government issue, it could not be sold by the post office or postal employees. Bissell continued to plead with the man until he finally gave her permission to set up a stand in the post office lobby.

Emily enthusiastically set up shop. To explain the seals' mission, she printed a note on each envelope filled with the colorful stamps.

*25 Christmas Stamps and sold for a penny a piece to
    stamp out the White Plague.
Put this stamp with message bright on every Christmas letter;
Help the tuberculosis fight, and make the New Year better.
These stamps do not carry any kind of mail,
but any kind of mail will carry them.*

Emily thought that everyone would be willing to pay a penny to obtain twenty-five beautiful seals to affix to their holiday mailings. Yet she would quickly discover that the public was not ready for the concept. On December 7, 1907, she manned a booth in the post office but raised only $25. The next day sales dropped, and by the third day, no one was buying them. Even when she spoke to civic groups and church groups, few responded. Without outside help, Emily realized that her campaign was dead and the hospital would be forced to close before Christmas.

Taking her fight to a larger battlefield, Emily hopped a train to Philadelphia. When she arrived in the City of Brotherly Love, she went directly to the North American, one of Philadelphia's leading newspapers. The Sunday editor listened but declined to act. He thought his readers would frown upon linking the beautiful Christmas holidays with a disease too gruesome to discuss.

Depressed and defeated, Emily was ready to give up. As she wearily rose from her seat and made her way back through the newspaper's offices, she spied staff columnist Leigh Mitchell

Hodges. On a whim, she stopped at the man's desk and told him her story. She then pulled out a sheet of seals for the writer to view. When he saw the colorful stamps, Hodges's eyes lit up. Here was a cause that he felt called to join.

Somehow Hodges managed to get the editor to see the vision and rethink his position. "Tell Miss Bissell the *North American* is hers for the holidays," the head man told the columnist. "Drop what you're doing and give this your whole time. Take all the space you need. Ask her to send fifty thousand seals to our offices by tomorrow."

Hodges's story appeared the next day with the banner headline "Stamp Out Tuberculosis." The paper had not even hit the streets when the first package of seals was purchased by a tiny, poorly dressed newsboy. When asked why he would give a penny for the seals, the youth replied, "Me sister's got it."

The first 50,000 seals were quickly sold, and another 50,000 were printed. Buyers included President Theodore Roosevelt, the Chief Justice of the Supreme Court, and the Speaker of the House of Representatives. By the time the holiday season was over, $3000 had been raised and the small Delaware clinic had been saved.

The following year the American Red Cross backed the seals and made the colorful stamps one of its national campaigns. In 1908 Americans purchased more than $135,000 worth of the Christmas Seals. In 1917 the total topped a million dollars for the first time.

Before his death in 1927, Einar Holboell, the man whose

love and compassion first linked Christmas to the need to help those suffering from TB, was knighted by the king of Denmark for his contributions to the cause. Holboell was also honored by scores of other countries, including the United States, for his vision and his work.

Emily Bissell continued to raise money for Christmas Seals until she died just after World War II at the age of eighty-seven. She lived long enough to see her holiday passion become the action that cured millions.

The American Lung Association still relies heavily on Christmas Seals to help fund education, advocacy, and research programs about asthma, tobacco use, and air quality. Today more than forty nations have made Christmas Seals one of their most important holiday traditions. A person can now even purchase an e-mail Christmas Seal. Thanks to this seemingly tiny part of the holiday season, hundreds of thousands of people have lived to experience the joy of Christmas. Their second chance at life is due to common people remembering the real reason for the season, the essence of the lessons Christ taught—that reaching out to the "least of these" is the ultimate act of Christian faith and the most important expression of Christmas love and goodwill.

~9~

CHRISTMAS TREES

Universal acceptance of the Christmas tree as a holiday essential occurred less than two centuries ago, but the roots of bringing an evergreen into one's home during the darkest days of Christmas can be traced back more than one thousand years. The evergreen tree, along with the Christ child and Santa Claus, has evolved into a central symbol of the world's most celebrated holiday. To Christians, the Christmas tree is often more than just another decoration; it is a vibrant part of the spiritual essence of the season as well.

Even a thousand years after the crucifixion of Christ, most of those living in what is now Scandinavia had not been reached by Christian missionaries. In the winter, with the winds howling, snow piled up as high as rooftops, and temperatures constantly hovering below zero, life was tough. Scores of villagers and animals died each year due to the effects of this dark and depressing season. Yet during the long and often brutal winter, when the sun disappeared for months and nights seemed to last forever, the deeply superstitious Vikings found hope and strength in the evergreen tree. The evergreen not only survived the harsh winter; it even seemed to thrive when times were most bleak. In an effort to bring some of the magic of the evergreen tree into their lives, Vikings would chop down a fir and place it in their homes. Having a tree in the house was said to bring the gift of strength to live through the worst stretches of winter.

The Vikings were not the only ones who considered the evergreen a symbol of life and good fortune. Many other people groups throughout Europe incorporated into their lives the mystery of this tree that stayed green in winter. The evergreen even became a central theme in many pagan cultures' worship practices.

In the seventh century, St. Boniface, a monk from Crediton, Devonshire, England, constantly traveled across Europe as a missionary. On his many treks, the dynamic Boniface established hundreds of Christian churches throughout France and Germany. It has been written that on a trip to central Europe he came across a band of men who had gathered around a huge oak tree. One of these men held in his hands a small boy who had been chosen as a sacrifice to the god Thor. When he saw what was transpiring, Boniface demanded that the men stop their ritual. When they refused, the priest walked up to the old tree and struck the trunk with his fist. In an act the men viewed as a miracle, the mighty oak shuddered and then fell to the ground. As the dust settled, a tiny fir tree became visible just behind where the oak had towered. Boniface pointed the tree out to the men, explaining that the evergreen was the Tree of Life. He told them that the tree even winter could not kill stood for the eternal life offered to them by Christ. Finally he pointed to the triangular shape of the tree and stated that the fir's three points represented the Holy Trinity of God the Father, Son, and Holy Ghost. Each of the men supposedly gave their lives to Christ at the spot where the tiny evergreen grew.

Five centuries later this story had become a legend, and each winter throughout France and Germany, evergreen trees were hung from ceilings as a symbol of Christianity. Though history does not tell us why, the firs were always hung upside down. This practice would continue for another two hundred years.

Besides being hung in homes during the Dark Ages, in much of the Baltic region of Europe evergreen trees were cut and placed outside Catholic churches during the month of December. These firs were referred to as "paradise trees" and were used by the clergy to explain the story of Adam and Eve to children. Apples were hung on the trees, representing the fruit of knowledge. Children playing the parts of Adam and Eve would listen to another child portraying the serpent and then proceed to eat the apple. When they took a bite, they were chased from church property into the cold, cruel world. The fir was used for this pageant because its everlasting nature represented the eternal life that God offers through belief in his son, Jesus. Thus, the final facet of the lesson was that human beings could repent and be welcomed back into the presence of God. While not a recognized Christmas symbol, the paradise tree did move an ancient pagan custom another step toward becoming a tradition rooted in Christian faith.

Probably the first fir that was actually called a Christmas tree was put up in Latvia, a Baltic country in northern Europe, in 1510. It was a small tree set on a table rather than hung from the ceiling. In 1521 Princess Helene de Mecklembourg, who was familiar with the use of Christmas trees in Latvia, married the Duke of Orleans. When she moved to France, she introduced the Christmas tree to Paris. Yet this act only put the Christmas tree in the castle, not on the map. By the late 1500s, the practice of displaying paradise trees had been largely forgotten, and fir trees had been taken down from ceilings and placed on floors. Trees were not yet generally associated with Christmas, however, but were considered throwbacks to pagan rituals. It would take one of history's most famous Christian leaders to change that perception.

Legend has it that Martin Luther was walking home on a dark December evening when he was struck by the beauty of the starlight coming through the branches of the many fir trees in the woods around his home. The German Protestant Reformer was so captivated by the way the filtered light appeared that he felt moved to duplicate this effect on the tree he had placed in his home. He tied a candleholder onto one of the evergreen's branches, put a candle in the wooden holder, and lit it. Walking to the opposite side of the tree, he studied the flickering light. He liked the effect and attached several more candles in the same way. Not only was the preacher's family impressed, so were his neighbors. A host of them added candles to their own indoor trees, and the tradition of a lighted tree was born.

Luther taught his friends and family that the tree represented the everlasting love of God. He pointed out that the evergreen's color did not fade, just as the Lord's love would not fade, no matter what the circumstance or trial. The candlelight represented the hope that Christ brought to the world through his birth and resurrection. Thus, to those who knew Luther, the tree evolved into a symbol not just of Christmas but of Christian faith in general.

During the American Revolution, Hessian mercenaries fighting for the Colonial army introduced the Christmas tree to the United States. The idea of using trees during the holidays, however, did not catch on and returned to Germany with the soldiers. It was Pennsylvania Germans who finally brought the Christmas tree to America to stay in the 1820s. Yet most Americans not of German descent associated Christmas trees with German culture and didn't think to make it part of their own tradition. That changed in 1841 when Germany's Prince Albert wed England's Queen Victoria and introduced the ancient German tradition to London's Windsor Castle. Several years later an engraving of the royal couple's Christmas tree appeared in American newspapers. And the timing could not have been better. Americans were just beginning to open up to the concept of celebrating Christ's birth.

In the days before the Civil War, there was a new spirit of Christmas in the United States. The idea of a tree being brought into the home to heighten the sense of the wonder of Christmas immediately appealed to both the wealthy and the country's growing middle class. It quickly became a tradition even in the poorest homes as a cedar tree could easily be found in fields and cost nothing. It seemed that a Christmas tree was one of the few things that every American could afford.

Up until 1851, anyone who wanted a Christmas tree had to travel out to the woods to cut their own. As America was still a very rural society, this was easy for most people. Yet for some New Yorkers, trapped in the city, it was all but impossible. A businessman, Mark Carr, saw opportunity knocking. Just before Christmas, Carr took a huge horse-drawn sled into the Catskills, chopped down scores of ever-greens, and hauled them back to New York City. He set the trees out in a vacant lot and sold them. Soon Christmas-tree lots could be found in every major American city, and the idea of marketing Christmas trees migrated back to Europe.

By the 1880s, Christmas trees were so popular that many worried the seasonal rush to obtain them would make fir trees extinct. Artificial trees, made out of feathers or brushes, were introduced as an alternative. Though it would take some time, the idea eventually caught on. But even in our modern age, real trees remain the most popular Christmas symbol in the world.

The Christmas tree is the most endearing of all the holiday traditions that originated in pagan cultures. Christmas trees can be found in stores and churches, on streets and in yards, in schools and businesses, and of course, in hundreds of millions of homes around the world. For many, the tree that can survive even the most barbarous winter has come to represent the everlasting promise of eternal life offered through Christ. The lights placed on the tree represent the light that the babe in the manger brought to a dark and hopeless world. Because the evergreen is so strong and so resilient, it has also come to represent peace and hope to millions.

~ 10 ~

THE COLORS OF CHRISTMAS

In the song "Silver Bells," written for the Bob Hope movie *The Lemon-Drop Kid* in 1951, the streetlights are decked out for the holidays because they blink "a bright red and green." Today, with the addition of yellow for caution, these same traffic signals now flash bright red, gold, and green. By doing so, they fully represent the pigments that have come to be the most visible in what is undoubtedly the most colorful time of the year.

Why are green, red, and gold generally thought of as the colors of Christmas? While there are many stories and legends surrounding the use of this trio of hues, in truth no one knows why or when these colors were chosen. No one has stepped forward to claim credit for deciding that these three colors would be assigned for holiday use, but when judged on their historic symbolism, green, red, and gold simply best define Christmas. It would be all but impossible to think of the holidays without them.

In the more than 2000 years since the birth of Christ, many colors—such as white, purple, and blue—have found their way into the spectrum of the season, but the trio of signal-light colors reigns. These three colors were not just haphazardly splashed on the canvas of the season but were born out of existing holiday customs combined with a knowledge of the story of Jesus' life.

The first hue to be linked with Christmas was probably green. Long before Christ was born, green had been a powerful symbol of mystery and life. Ancient cultures observed the fir trees and holly bushes growing in the midst of the harshest winters and were fascinated. When all other plants had died or grown barren, the people of the woods believed that some type of magical power had to be fueling these evergreens' survival. Because of this flourishing life when there seemed only to be death, these green survivors were both worshiped and feared. Some folks felt that evil had given the evergreen plants the power to evade the natural order of the seasons. Others taught that the gods had breathed life into them to preserve a bit of beauty during the bleak days of winter. While early humankind did not comprehend what made these plants live year-round, most cultures, especially in Europe, came to think of green as the color of life.

During the feasts of the winter solstice, evergreen holly was woven into wreaths in Rome. As the Romans celebrated the passing of the shortest day of the year and looked forward to the "rebirth" of the sun and the return of warm weather, holly could be seen everywhere. It hung from doors and on the walls of homes and was even sold in shops. In the fourth century, when the church decided to celebrate Christ's birth on December 25th (which happened to be the final day of the annual celebration of the sun god Saturn), many Christians who had used holly to decorate for the Roman festival left the green sprays in place for Christmas as well. Thus, over time, holly and its green color came to be linked with Christ's birth. A few legends even placed this bush or tree near Jesus as he lay in the manger.

As green represented the life associated with the birth of Christ, red would come to represent his death on the cross. With such dark symbolism, this might seem a strange color to add to the Christmas bouquet. Yet as important as the first chapter of the story of Jesus' life was, it was how his life on earth ended that made the events in Bethlehem really important.

While holly leaves are always green, ancient civilizations were probably most fascinated by the red berries that sprang forth from the holly plants in the darkest days of winter. How could this plant not only live but also produce fruit when no other plants could? In the minds of most folks living in ancient times, the only answer was magic.

As the holly became associated with Christmas, church leaders began to look for a way to erase the pagan myths that surrounded the plant and replace them with analogies that reflected the beauty, power, and truth of the Christian faith. Thus, the red berries that appeared when everything in the world seemed dead represented the blood of Christ and the eternal life that could belong to anyone who chose to accept the Lord as Savior. While green represented new life, red came to symbolize the reason for Christ's coming to earth, dying, and then rising from the dead.

Another plant that locked in the use of red at Christmas in America was the poinsettia. This Mexican plant looked to be just another green leafy growth that blended in with a large array of other native plants—until just before Christmas, when a host of the poinsettia's leaves broke out in a shockingly brilliant scarlet.

But it was probably a bishop's robes that fully entrenched red as the second most important color of the holiday season. By the Middle Ages, the legend of St. Nicholas, the cleric from the Dark Ages who often gave gifts to children in his church district, had become a very important part of December throughout Eastern Europe. In stories and paintings Nicholas was almost always dressed in red robes, which would prompt those who invented Santa Claus in the early 1800s to outfit the jolly old elf in red as well. With this final addition, a scarlet hue had been permanently affixed to the holiday season in every corner of the world.

The third color always seen during the holidays probably has the clearest association to the Christian faith. One of the gifts the wise men brought to the baby Jesus was gold, so this valuable and shiny metal was linked to Christmas before almost anything else could be. Gold was also the color associated with wealth and royalty. Certainly the Son of God was worthy of a tribute in gold. It seems appropriate that the man who would someday be mocked as "King of the Jews" would be associated with the color of the crowns that graced royal heads of state.

Yet in the case of Christmas, gold also came to signify light. A bright star, shining down on the earth, guided the wise men with its golden beam. This light would come to represent the illumination that Christ brought to the world with his teachings and by his example. And as gold was the most precious gift on earth, it fit well with Christ's mission. After all, through the gift of his own life, Christ would give humankind a way to experience eternal life in a place where the very streets are said to be paved with gold.

Green, red, and gold are the three colors that announce the return of the Christmas season each year. Yet they are more than rich colors; they represent the rich history of the most celebrated holiday on earth. With green representing life that remains vital and beautiful even during the darkest trials, red symbolizing the blood that was shed so human souls could be reconciled to God, and gold promising the gift of eternal life, these colors ring true at Christmastime and throughout the year. If you look hard enough, the spirit of Christ and Christmas can always be seen in the colors that make up the annual holiday rainbow.

~ 11 ~

DECORATIONS AND
ORNAMENTS

Christmas decorations, though usually thought of as a companion to the Christmas tree, actually predate the widespread use of fir-tree displays in the home. Holly was probably the first Christmas decoration, a carryover from the Roman use of the plant during the winter solstice festivals. Other evergreens associated with pagan ceremonies, such as fir trees and mistletoe, soon joined the waxy bush's branches in Christian holiday celebrations. But handmade ornaments and decorations did not appear until the beginning of the Middle Ages. So for more than a thousand years, the holidays were not very festive or bright.

During the cold and foreboding days of winter, when the harsh weather drove those in northern Europe inside their homes, Scandinavians used straw to make stars, crowns, angels, and even manger scenes. The Vikings had begun this artistic exercise as a way of honoring their pagan gods, and as they converted to the Christian faith, they adapted their craft to fit into their very spiritual celebration of the Christmas season. These simple, fragile decorations of the Dark Ages were probably the first ornaments that expressed the themes of Christmas. Even now it is easy to imagine what a straw angel set on a tiny wooden table must have meant to a child of the time. Of course, that child could not have guessed that that object of wonder would be the humble beginning of a billion-dollar industry.

At about the same time that Norse men and women were working with straw, Germans and Italians began creating wooden frames shaped like triangles. Made with shelves that gave the frames as many as five or six different levels, these pyramid-like fabrications were constructed to either hang on the wall on sit on a table. Those who built them brought these display frames out each Christmas season and placed candles, wooden carvings, tiny paintings, and small trinkets on the shelves. In time these frames, called *litchstocks* in Germany and ceppos in Italy, grew in popularity to the point where they could be found in the homes of everyone from royalty to peasant.

Eventually, hand-carved manger scenes were placed on such frames, with the baby Jesus lying on the top shelf and a star affixed to the tip of the frame's highest point. As the popularity of the *litchstocks* and *ceppos* grew, many skilled artists began to sell or trade them. Therefore, these decorations were probably the first that had commercial value.

These nativity figures in frames led to the carving of larger wooden figures for freestanding manger displays, which were used to adorn tables in homes and churches. The wooden nativity sets were passed down from generation to generation and became treasured family heirlooms. Some were hand-painted, and scores of families began a tradition of adding a new piece to their display each year. With triangle frames and nativity displays firmly entrenched as holiday traditions, other similar items followed.

By the time of the Reformation, Christmas trees were beginning to be an important facet of the holiday season in German homes. Red apples were the first decorations affixed to these trees and were soon joined by candles, strings of popcorn, white candy canes, cookies, and even dolls and small toys. During the 1850s, when Christmas trees began to be part of the holiday tradition in England and the United States, the popcorn strings were often tinted with food coloring, and cookies were sometimes cut into the shapes of stars and angels. Strings of paper chains and homemade drawings were also hung on many trees. Because each family had different degrees of artistic talent and varied interests and beliefs, most of the world's hundreds of thousands of Christmas trees had a unique appearance. Yet the homemade nature of ornaments and the individuality of Christmas decorations would soon change dramatically. As it did, the holiday season would move outside the home and into the marketplace.

When a family cut their tree down and brought it into the house, limbs were often cut off in an attempt to make the tree more uniform in shape or to fit it into a room. Not wanting to waste these cuttings, inventive Germans wove the limbs into Christmas wreaths. Often hung on the doors as a sign of welcome, this greenery was usually adorned with small wooden carvings, a hand-painted sign of holiday greeting, or a figure from a wooden or tin nativity scene. Soon inspired woodmen began to sell fully decorated wreaths. While weaving the limbs was easy work for most of them, creating the art to adorn the boughs was a skill few possessed. With the advent of wreaths and trees, there was now a market for ornaments.

The first commercial ornaments were produced by a German company, Lauscha, in the 1860s. Inspired by the paper chains and popcorn strings children made, Lauscha produced garlands made of glass beads. The company also created tin figures that could be hung on trees. Both of these items were so popular that the line was soon expanded to include glass ornaments, which, unlike the first two products, required the skills of true artisans.

Lauscha used highly skilled craftsmen and clay molds to create the first glass ornaments. At the company's plant, located deep in Germany's Thuringian Forest, the artisans began the process of forming an ornament by heating a glass tube over a flame, inserting the tube into a clay mold, and then blowing air through the tube to expand the glass into the shape of the mold. Initially, the molds were shaped only like nuts and fruits.

After the glass was allowed to cool, a silver nitrate solution was swirled into it. This silvering technique, developed in the 1850s by Justus von Liebig, gave the ornament a bright silver finish. When seen in the proper light, it even appeared to glow. After the nitrate solution dried, the ornament was hand-painted. Finally it was topped with a metal cap that had a small hook or loop. When a string or wire was attached to this cap, the glass figure could be tied to a tree.

An immediate hit in Germany, glass ornaments were exported to England and, a decade later, to the United States. American manufacturers soon began producing their own ornaments. The first American-made glass ornaments were created by William DeMuth in New York around 1870.

In 1880 Frank W. Woolworth was advertising and selling Lauscha glass ornaments. Woolworth had opened his first "five-cent" store in Utica, New York, one year earlier. By 1910, Woolworth's five-and-dimes had become a coast-to-coast operation, with more than a thousand retail outlets. Frank Woolworth's impact on the holidays was huge. A generous man of faith who was the first employer to give Christmas bonuses to his workers, he probably also did more to commercialize Christmas than any other person in history.

Other stores in the late 1800s also filled their shelves in December with glass decorations. New suppliers jumped on board, and the competition to create the latest design was often heated. In a world where most families added only a single ornament per year to their collection and the sales window was only a few weeks each year, developing an ornament that stood apart from a competitor's offering was especially important.

Of all the new companies to jump into ornament production, another German company was viewed as having developed the best and most influential of the new holiday designs. Dresden fiberboard ornaments were handmade, double sided, embossed, and die cut, usually on gold or silver metallic paper. Much more durable than glass ornaments, these decorations appealed to those who had children or limited ways to store fragile glass ornaments. Dresden and other similar companies cut into the Christmas-ornament market, yet glass was still the industry standard. During this period the most popular ornaments were simple red balls.

Around 1890, as standards of living rose and the middle class grew, English and American consumers began demanding more and more decorations for their trees. Homemade decorations had fallen out of fashion, and ornament makers were hard pressed to keep up with the great demand. Thanks to the rush to cover Christmas trees with all the trimmings that could possibly be found, Christmas was suddenly big business.

By the turn of the century, Woolworth was annually importing more than 200,000 glass ornaments. Because the company bought in such huge volumes, it was able to offer common ornaments for just a dime. As decorations were so cheap, suddenly even those who were considered poor or lower middle class could put up holiday displays in their homes. Sales from Christmas decorations in 1900 topped $25 million in Woolworth's stores alone. Whereas twenty years earlier only a handful of design molds were being used to create a dozen different glass ornaments, now there were nearly 10,000 molds. Bells, angels, snowflakes, and Santa Clauses joined fruit, nuts, and balls—and more shapes were added each year. With the invention and sale of Christmas-tree lights, the industry really took off. Nothing, not even a global war, could stop its extraordinary growth.

During World War I, the importing of ornaments from Lauscha was halted. Scores of new American companies stepped in to fill the void. Though the glass ornaments produced in the states didn't match the artistry of the German ornaments, most consumers didn't care. They purchased all they could find. And because these ornaments were easily broken, most buyers came back year after year.

Though ornament makers constantly embraced new themes and experimented with different colors, Christmas-tree ornaments stayed pretty much the same until 1937. In 1937 Max Eckardt, an importer of German glass ornaments, perceived that another major war was on the horizon. Fearing that the coming war would ruin him financially, he began his own glassworks business. Joining with Corning, Eckardt's Shiney Brite Company produced something new and exciting: mass-market, high-quality, brightly colored glass ornaments. Best of all, they were very inexpensive.

The development of new compounds during World War II, especially plastic and new metals, changed the face of Christmas decorations in the 1950s. Producing intricate ornaments in volume was no longer difficult. So in an era when the prices of most things went up, the cost of Christmas decorations came down dramatically. As the cost was reduced, Christmas decorations moved beyond the tree and were featured throughout the home, even spilling into people's yards.

Previously, only businesses had used lights and decorations on the outside of buildings. But by the 1960s and 1970s, whole neighborhoods were flashing seasonal cheer with lighted nativity displays, plastic Santas perched on roofs, and angels seemingly suspended in midair. With these yard displays, a new tradition was started. For millions of people, Christmas was no longer complete until everyone had loaded into the family car to drive around town and view the outdoor exhibits created by friends and neighbors. Naturally these displays inspired others to get involved, and outdoor decorations became as important to the industry as Christmas-tree decorations.

Today the Christmas-decoration industry ranks behind only gifts in seasonal sales. A large number of people spend days decorating their homes and yards with thousands of lights and displays. In almost every corner of the United States, as well as across Europe, holiday decor spectaculars fill stores.

The Norse Christians who first shaped straw in the form of an angel knew that what they had created was an expression of their faith. Families who decorated some of the early

Christmas trees with strings of popcorn and homemade ornaments saw their family's faith, personality, and unity in the final results. Do our Christmas decorations today reveal these same things about us? Most people would say no. But perhaps the family that works for so many hours setting up complicated yard exhibits and elaborate home displays is bonding in a way similar to those who trimmed trees with homemade decorations in earlier times. And there is no doubt that the efforts of today's families bring joy and wonder to those who stop and look at what has been created in so many homes and yards.

While Christmas decorations have definitely changed through the years, the essence of Christmas is still clearly visible. In millions of homes today, just as in generations past, children look forward to placing the star or angel on top of the tree and flipping the switch that turns on the Christmas-tree lights. And just like the straw angel of ancient Christmas, a simple ornament still holds great emotional and spiritual value for millions of people.

Christmas decorations may not bring peace on earth, but they do create a lot of joy in the world.

~ 12 ~

EPIPHANY

Most people have heard the word "epiphany," but few Americans have a full understanding of its meaning. In modern terminology, epiphany is defined as "an intuitive grasp of reality usually through something simple and striking, an illuminating discovery, a revealing scene or moment." In simpler language, it means "to show, to make known, or to reveal." But what was the revealing moment that generated an important Christian holiday? Why has Epiphany been celebrated almost as long as Christmas and Easter, and how do the important events that are remembered on this day relate to the celebration of Christmas?

Most Christian cultures teach that when the wise men, or Magi, completed their journey and located Jesus, an epiphany transpired. Many people consider this event to be the initial manifestation of Christ as Savior and King. The fact that foreigners, who probably knew little of the Jewish faith, traveled so far to honor this baby seems to foreshadow Jesus' great mission to be "a light for revelation" to all people (Luke 2:25–32). Maybe that is why Epiphany, little known as a Christian holy day in America, is so important to many Christians through-out Europe, Latin America, and elsewhere that they believe the events that transpired on this day are more consequential to the Christian faith than even the day of Christ's birth.

In the fourth century the era's most celebrated preacher, Augustine, so romanticized and embellished the story of the Epiphany that he almost ruined it. In the famous preacher's ver-sion of Epiphany, the gift-bearing Magi were bestowed with an upgraded social standing. Augustine made them members of the royalty, kings if you will. This embellishment created an even larger problem in connection with the secular celebrations of Christ's birth. Many Christians still observed Christmas as the Romans had celebrated the winter solstice, with drinking and raucous parties, and with Epiphany, the clerics hoped to mark a new, more inspired holiday. The thinking was that Epiphany would pave the way for a more religious commem-oration of the events of Jesus' birth. Yet because of the Magi's new claim to royal blood, Augustine's legendary version of the day of revelation eventually backfired on the church.

In many places Epiphany was literally taken over by mem-bers of the royal families. A host of blue bloods completely bought into Augustine's legend that the wise men were actually monarchs. Kings, queens, and others in their families embraced this retelling of the Magi's trip as if it were the gos-pel truth. They therefore saw Epiphany as a day to celebrate themselves, their role in society, and Christ's supposed close association with the world's monarchs. Plus, as people who obviously held such a place of honor in God's world, it afforded the rulers an opportunity to be honored by their subjects.

Hence, on January 6th, the day designated as Epiphany, kings, queens, dukes, duchesses, and other members of the ruling class put on their finest clothing and staged huge parties to celebrate the arrival of their ancestors at the nativity scene. This meant that the day was filled with the type of events that had typified pagan festivals in the royal castle: singing, dancing, plays, magic acts, and even games of chance. Thanks to Augustine's invention of the kings from the East, in almost every country Epiphany slowly mutated from a time to recognize the real meaning of the wise men's gifts to Jesus into a day when all bowed before earthly monarchs and paid tribute to these guardians of the state. By the Middle Ages, in much of the European world, Epiphany had evolved into something more like Mardi Gras than a holy day of Christian worship. And by this time, the holiday was probably better known as King's Day or Twelfth Night than it was Holy Epiphany.

After a while the celebrations of Epiphany grew as unruly as the riots that characterized Christmas Day. In some countries, mock kings were chosen through a vote or by wagering. The main job of these mock kings, known as the Kings of Misrule, was to lead the masses in toast after toast to whatever and whomever they chose. Needless to say, the wise men were rarely acknowledged during the festivities and the church was put on the back burner on the very day when the universality of the Christian faith could have been made most clear.

Thanks in large part to Prince Albert and Queen Victoria, Christmas in England and America finally became a festive family time in the mid-1800s. It's ironic that it took a royal family to toss royalty out of Epiphany and make January 6th a holiday to celebrate the revelation of the Magi. Epiphany was considered the final day of the holiday season, which ran from Christmas Eve to the Eve of Epiphany, and in its new form, Epiphany became a time to once again gather as a family, take down the decorations and trees, and sing carols. With this transformation, Epiphany had finally become what the fourth-century church leaders had wanted: a spiritual holiday.

On the Eve of Epiphany church services were held; prayers were said; dried herbs were baked or simmered, filling homes with the pungent smell of spices; and the letters C, M, and B were written above the doors of many houses. It was said that these letters represented the names of the Magi: Caspar, Melchior, and Balthasar. In truth no one knows how many wise men made the journey to find Jesus, much less what their names were; like Augustine's kings, these names were simply an invention. Today scholars believe that the letters originally stood for the Latin *Christus mansionem benedictat*, which means "Christ bless this home." That meaning was evidently lost over the years, and as the wise men were given fictional names, many who wrote the letters believed them to be a welcoming sign for the wise men themselves. In other words, this was an ancient version of the signs children place in yards today that say "Santa Please Stop Here."

Children would put out food for the Magi and hay for the wise men's horses; then they would anxiously go to bed. The next morning the little ones hurried outside to see if the wise men had come and taken their offerings. Usually the food had disappeared and had been replaced by gold coins. Many people in England and America continued to celebrate Epiphany in this fashion until the end of the 1800s, when the new tradition of Santa Claus, or Father Christmas, moved almost all gift giving to December 25th. The celebration of Epiphany began to wane, and the wise men became just another facet of Christmas pageants, cards, and songs such as "We Three Kings." Yet in many other nations, Epiphany was not lost and is still an important part of the holidays.

In areas influenced by German customs, on January 6th children dress up as the Magi, follow a child who holds a large star, and travel door to door until they find the home that has been designated as the place where the baby Jesus is staying. The children then leave monetary gifts that they have collected or that have been given by their church. These gifts are later passed along to the sick and the poor.

In Argentina, Venezuela, Puerto Rico, and most areas of Mexico, where Epiphany is still usually called King's Day, the wise men leave presents on the Eve of Epiphany, just as they did more than two thousand years ago for the Christ child. And in most of these nations, a "king's cake" is baked and eaten on January 6th.

In Spain and Italy many children leave out shoes filled with barley for the Magi's animals. According to an ancient legend, a kindly witch named La Befana, who missed the trip with the Magi to the manger, now accompanies the wise men and leaves gifts for children. In many seaport communities in Spain, a boat comes into the harbor on the morning of Epiphany and the Magi disembark. The three men then parade through the streets, sharing greetings of goodwill and giving candy to the children who line the parade route.

The churches in the United States and Britain that still observe Epiphany have recently been trying to restore the day's original meaning. These congregations teach that the anniversary of the arrival of the wise men is a time to focus on the real mission of the Christian faith and its body of believers. In worship services people discover that Epiphany is a time to put aside cultural, racial, and social differences and recognize that Jesus came to offer salvation to all people. Hence, the holiday is again taking on a sense of the brotherhood that Christ tried to bring to the world during his life. If Epiphany can be revived, it might well become the answer to a long-wished-for holiday that reflects reverently on the birth of Jesus. As a bookend to Christmas, it could become the vessel that puts a truly spiritual cap on the holiday season.

13

GIFTS

After Jesus was born in Bethlehem in Judea, during the time of King Herod, Magi from the east came to Jerusalem and asked, 'Where is the one who has been born king of the Jews? We saw his star in the east and have come to worship him. . . .' On coming to the house, they saw the child with his mother Mary, and they bowed down and worshiped him. Then they opened their treasures and presented him with gifts of gold and of incense and of myrrh" (Matt. 2:1–2, 11).

Even today everyone knows that gold is one of the most sought-after treasures on earth. At the time of Christ's birth this precious metal might have even been even more highly prized. A gift of gold meant that the gift was very important and that the person who received the gift was a loved one or a person of very high standing. To give gold to a baby would have been all but unheard of, unless, of course, that child was a king. The wise men had to have been given divine insight into the future work of Jesus to be moved to present the child with this gift. They must have known that the gold would be used to support the most important work the world would ever know.

The wise man who brought frankincense was bringing an important symbol of worship, thus implying that he knew that this child was a central figure in God's plans. At the time of Christ's birth the frankincense tree was considered so sacred that only those pure of heart and mind were allowed to come near it. The giver must have known that this tree would have welcomed the Christ child. Frankincense was made from the sap of the tree and was an ingredient in the oil used for religious anointing. It was also burned during special offerings. This giver must have believed that the incense foreshadowed Christ's mission on earth.

Myrrh, a resin used in burial ceremonies, was rare and very costly. Myrrh was the most unique gift the wise men presented to Christ. Today this gift would be something akin to bringing a coffin as a present for a baby shower. Why was this sweet smelling "death spice" given along with gold and frankincense? The Bible does not say. But many believe this gift was a sign that the wise men understood the secret of this newborn king's life, work, and death. Whether or not the myrrh was kept and used for Christ's burial thirty-three years later is unknown, but it might have been.

Most people today trace the practice of giving gifts on Christmas Day to the three gifts that the Magi gave to Jesus. Certainly these gifts, as well as the long and perilous journey the givers made, are wonderful examples of giving and sacrifice for today's Christians. Yet how three wise men paying tribute to the Son of God evolved into a practice that has restructured the retail industry worldwide is a complicated story that evolved over the next nineteen hundred years.

Even before Christ was born, gifts were exchanged during the Roman ceremonies of Saturnalia. Throughout these ancient winter-solstice holidays, people traded presents, believing their generosity would bring them good fortune in the coming year. During the first few centuries of Christianity, new Christian converts often continued to celebrate the old Roman holidays and traditions, which meant they bought and exchanged gifts during Saturnalia. By the fourth century, when December 25th was designated as the day to remember Christ's birth, the celebration of Saturnalia was beginning to wind down. Since the official date of Christmas fell during the same period as the old Roman holiday, it was only natural that some Christians carried over the practice of gift giving as they celebrated Christ's birth. It would make a wonderful story if the gift-giving practice of these early Christians was the foundation of today's holiday custom, but it is not. During this time, gift giving and Christmas did not fully connect, and the practice all but died out as the holiday of Saturnalia was abandoned.

A Roman tradition that was continued during this period, however, was the practice of giving a New Year's gift. Gift exchanges on the first day of the year continued through the Dark Ages and Middle Ages and right up until the rule of

Queen Victoria. This gift-giving tradition eventually merged into the tradition of giving presents during the Christmas season, but it took several other events to make that union a reality.

The legend of St. Nicholas, who became the bishop of Myra in the beginning of the fourth century, is the next link in the Christmas-gift chain. Legend has it that during his life the priest rode across Asia Minor bestowing gifts upon poor children. Santa Claus and Christmas stockings can be traced directly to the story of Nicholas's life. He was so highly respected and loved by those who knew him that the anniversary of his death, December 6th, became a day to present special gifts to children. So during the Middle Ages, St. Nicholas's Day was the most exciting day of the year to thousands of Christian children in eastern and central Europe.

While giving gifts to children was a noble gesture, many European rulers studied the Scripture concerning the Magi's gifts to Jesus, completely ignored the example of Nicholas, and turned the Scriptures around to suit their own selfish desires. Using the Bible as the rationale behind their demands, a host of the kings and queens in Europe wrote into law that subjects were to provide annual Christmas tributes to their rulers. Thus, the very poorest people in Europe were required to give the best they had to the richest family in the land each year on December 25th. Soon lesser royals and government appointees were demanding Christmas tributes as well. The poor were deliberately being taken advantage of in the name of the Christian faith. Even the church had to pay the rulers. So rather than making the holidays a time of celebration and joy, the demands of many of Europe's elite put Christmas gifts into a rather bad light.

In the tenth century a Bohemian duke, now remembered as King Wenceslas, began to change the practice of Christmas tributes. Rather than demanding gifts from his people, Wenceslas took on the role of the wise men. He roamed his kingdom during the holidays and distributed firewood, food, and clothing. The duke, reaching out to the least of those in his kingdom each year, inspired many in his land to do likewise.

On December 25, 1067, William the Conqueror also chose to reverse the accepted Christmas gift-giving tradition by donating a large sum of money to the pope. The actions of William and Wenceslas initiated change that would begin to take root first in Eastern Europe and much later in England and America.

During Martin Luther's era, Germans latched on to the examples found in the stories of St. Nicholas and Wenceslas. Many of them believed that Christmas gifts should be given anonymously. So the idea of secretly placing gifts out for friends and loved ones to find on Christmas jump-started the practice of giving Christmas gifts in Germany.

Soon the Dutch took this tradition a step further. They hid Christmas gifts and left notes that hinted at where the gifts could be found. By making the practice of receiving gifts into a game, the people of the Netherlands brought the excitement of the holidays directly to children.

The Danes took the game another step by wrapping gifts. Their unique tradition was to put a small, wrapped box into a larger one and continue to wrap and rewrap and box and rebox until the present was huge. In most cases there was a different name on each new layer of wrapping paper. Thus, the gift changed hands many times before it was finally fully unwrapped and given to the intended recipient.

The tradition of gift giving did not spread to England or to the New World during this period. In all regions under British rule, gifts, especially those for children, were not part of the Christmas season. This was partially due to the English history of a rowdy and irreverent holiday celebration. Yet the lack of gift giving in England at Christmastime was probably due mostly to the beliefs of the Puritans. While the children in Europe opened presents, Puritan children in England and America were taught that the wise men gave gifts only to Jesus, not to his family or to each other. Therefore, they reasoned, God did not want his Son's birthday to be a time of giving to anyone but Christ. He also did not want people to celebrate on this day, the Puritans argued. Christmas was to be a day of solemn reflection, not exultation. Thus, gifts were forbidden and would remain so until well after the American Revolution.

Christmas gifts were not part of the holiday season in the United States and England, but many people did receive gifts in the weeks after Christmas. New Year's gifts were common, especially among the upper class, just as they had been in Rome. Some families also gave small token gifts to children on January 6th—the "twelfth" or last day of Christmas, the day of Epiphany. Christians who followed the "Twelve Days of Christmas" gave presents on this day because they believed it to be the day—twelve days after Christ's birth—when the wise men arrived with their gifts. While gifts were exchanged in January in America, gift giving was still foreign to most as a Christmas tradition.

In the 1820s, when Clement Clarke Moore's poem "The Night Before Christmas" began to be widely distributed via magazines, newspapers, and later in books, everything changed. Suddenly children saw in writing that the presents were supposed to arrive on Christmas Eve or early in the morning on Christmas Day. Dickens's *A Christmas Carol* gave even more validity to this concept. Merchants, sensing potential profits, jumped on the bandwagon. Santa began to make appearances in stores, and in the years just after the Civil War, America became the center of the Christmas-gift-giving universe. Christmas presents caught on in England during the 1880s, and by the turn of the century, Christmas had replaced New Year's as the primary gift day of the year in Britain too. With Christmas taking over, the almost two-thousand-year-old practice of giving gifts on New Year's disappeared.

By 1900, with the advent of catalogs, large stores, depend-able mail service, and better-paying jobs, the Christmas season became the most important sales time of the year for most department stores. Thus, advertisers, toy makers, and clothing companies geared their most important campaigns and products for the month of December. Thanks largely to Christmas shopping, the Christmas season expanded to at least two weeks.

Buying gifts for soldiers fighting in a world war extended the Christmas season even more. During World War II, with men stationed halfway around the world from their homes, the post office declared that for troops to receive their Christmas presents on time, they would have to be mailed very early. In response, stores put up holiday displays even before the beginning of December, and the monthlong Thanksgiving-to-Christmas selling season arrived.

Today shoppers spend more than $4 billion per Christmas shopping day, or about $2.8 million each minute, during the holiday season in the United States alone. The average person in the United States spent more than $1000 on Christmas gifts in 2002. The Puritans would no doubt be appalled that Christmas gifts have become not only a driving force of the holidays but of the American economy as well. Yet there is much more to this custom than just dollars and cents.

While many think Christmas gift giving is rank com-mercialism and the cause of a great deal of stress, when put into proper perspective, these presents can open the door to teaching about the real meaning of the holidays. Christ was a king who came not to take, but to give. His gift was the ultimate sacrifice and therefore brings each Christmas gift into focus. While the custom of exchanging personal Christmas gifts is a relatively new tradition, it can easily be traced to some very enlightened men who believed that the birth of Jesus was worth a long, perilous journey to present the very best gifts they had to offer.

~ 14 ~
HANDEL'S MESSIAH

In August 1741, George Frideric Handel was at the end of his rope. He was fifty-six years old, in poor health, and near bankruptcy. The composer who had once been the top star in his field now found his name and fame all but forgotten. He was a has-been. His music was no longer played by the top orchestras in Europe. The man, looking like a hollow shell of what he had once been, hardly seemed capable of writing a simple song, much less the most powerful Christian music of all time. But in the midst of Handel's deep spiritual depression, events were set in motion that would trigger genius and bring Handel and his music into the bright beam of the spotlight forever. More important for Handel at that moment, these events would provide a way out of a miserable life that seemed to offer no hope.

With the wolves at his door, Handel was a deeply troubled man. He was concerned not only about his inability to create music for a new generation but also about his financial situation. He often confessed to friends that in his nightmares he saw himself spending his final days on earth in one of England's debtors' prisons. Worries of losing everything he had, coupled with his long list of health concerns, robbed him of sleep and energy. This in turn sapped his creativity. Each day became a mirror of the previous one, with the desperate composer praying for inspiration but coming up with no new ideas. To escape the anguish of where his life seemed to be heading, Handel often sought comfort in remembering the past—and that past was one of the most glorious in music history.

George Handel was born in Halle, Germany, on February 23, 1685. His interest in music developed even before he learned to read. Thanks largely to his mother's encouragement, he was given an education that included a great deal of vocal and instrumental instruction. Though obviously gifted, Handel flunked out of college. Yet in spite of his educational follies, the young man was determined to pursue a career in music. So he left home at eighteen and moved to Hamburg. For the next three years, he conducted an orchestra at the local opera house and played violin in another orchestra during ballet performances. At the age of twenty-one, influenced by the music around him, Handel wrote his first two operas.

Though his operas garnered some minor critical success, Handel was unable to find a secure niche in the Hamburg music scene. Sensing that he needed to be exposed to a wider variety of music, he pulled up stakes and moved to Italy in 1706. There the young composer would discover a musical genre that would in time make him one of the most famous men in all of Europe and lead to the creation of the most powerful Christian musical of all time.

In Italy, Handel wrote and presented two oratorios over the next three years. He was probably drawn to this musical form because of its popularity. These sacred pieces, written for choruses with strong soloists, were really little more than dramatic presentations that paraphrased stories from the Bible. Created to provide moral lessons for the audience, along with classical entertainment, oratorios closely resembled opera, minus the costumes and staging. Inexpensive to produce and easy to understand, oratorios were popular with both common people and the elite. Because they reflected his own faith and convictions, Handel loved these musical morality plays.

As Handel had a flair for composition, his oratorios stood apart from a host of other Italian composers' work, and he quickly gained a following among Italy's prestigious social set. With the backing of some of the best-known members of the royal family, his fame soon grew beyond Italy, and by the age of twenty-five, the former failed university student was a well-known composer throughout Europe. When he returned home to Germany in glory, Handel had become a hero to both his family and his friends.

While the German music establishment literally bowed before the young composer, the nation did not offer Handel the exposure and environment he felt he had to have to grow. The atmosphere in his native land seemed to stifle his creative juices. He needed and wanted a freer landscape to express his creativity. At twenty-six, Handel migrated to England. The move seemed earmarked for success when he struck gold almost as soon as he published his first piece in London.

Handel's English oratorios, presented in three acts, made him one of the most popular composers in London. Yet rather than limiting himself to crafting more oratorios, Handel continued to expand his reach by writing church and secular music, instrumental pieces, and operas, by creating new arrangements of past works, and by drafting exciting concertos. He even became the director of the Royal Academy of Music. For a while he was the most famous musician in England—the Elvis of his era—and the world sought him out, honoring him time and again with position and money. It seemed the only thing that could slow him down was illness. And it would ultimately be his health that would bring him to his knees and rob him of his glory and fame.

Even as a young man, Handel suffered from a wide variety of physical ailments. By the time he reached middle age, he was prone to strokes and fought long bouts with rheumatism. He was also close to blindness due to cataracts. Crude eye surgery only made the problem worse. The diseases that plagued his body also dried up his creative juices. Unable to produce additional popular works, Handel was all but destitute by August 1741. The fame that once brought the royal family to his home now could not purchase bread for his cupboard. Constantly racked by pain and partially paralyzed by another stroke, the grand master of music was praying to die before he suffered a fate he considered worse than death: being carted off to a debtors' jail. What he did not know nor could ever have guessed was that his opportunity for personal redemption was about to present itself in the simplest manner: a rap on the door.

Handel dreaded the knock of the mail carrier. His mail was rarely greetings from old friends, but rather a deluge of notes from bill collectors seeking payment. Yet on this warm day in August, the postman brought good news for a change, in the form of two letters.

The first hopeful letter Handel received was an invitation to perform again in Ireland. An old friend, the Duke of Devonshire, wanted the composer to come to Dublin and produce a series of benefit concerts "for the relief of the prisoners in the several gaols, and for the support of Mercer's Hospital in Stephen Street, and of the Charitable Infirmary on the Inn's Quay." Handel accepted the invitation as much to escape his creditors as to direct an orchestra again. While this first letter presented Handel the opportunity to perform and to escape his miserable existence in London, it was a second correspondence from a friend that provided the inspiration that would make the Irish performances unforgettable.

Charles Jennens was the kind of rich eccentric most folks avoided. He had a knack for messing up, constantly spouted foolish ideas, and always felt that his unique way of doing things was revolutionary. Most often his concepts were simply just bizarre. So a letter from Jennens would hardly be something that would excite the majority of those who knew him.

But Handel, broke and out of ideas, grabbed onto the correspondence with a zeal rare for a sick man. He remembered that Jennens had once written some good lyrics. Maybe, the composer thought, the man had done it again.

Jennens's letter was just what the doctor had ordered. Rather than inform Handel of a new idea or catch the composer up on the often comic routine of the eccentric's life, Jennens had sent a concept for a new oratorio. Essentially, he had reduced the Old Testament and New Testament stories of Christ to the passages he deemed the most important. It can be debated whether his efforts were genius or just a rehashing of others' work, but what cannot be doubted was the effect they had on Handel. The passages Jennens had selected revived and inspired Handel. He set his problems aside and in the next twenty-four days wrote what would become the most familiar oratorio of all time. It would also become one of the world's most beloved spiritual pieces and a Christmas tradition unlike any other.

It was on August 22 that Handel locked himself in his study and set to work. In seven days he created the first segment of his new oratorio, now known as the "Christmas" section of the *Messiah*. The next part, "The Redemption Story," took nine days to compose. Part three, "The Resurrection and Future Reign of Christ on Heaven and Earth," took another week. Polishing the piece many times over the next few months, Handel grew so pleased with it that he took the oratorio with him to Dublin.

On April 8, 1742, Handel began rehearsals of his newest musical work. He probably saw the oratorio not as a grand project but as an intimate experience between the listener and the Lord. Because of this thinking, he chose to work with only a handful of singers and a small orchestra. He wanted to keep the *Messiah* tight and focused. On April 13, the composer brought the work to life in front of a large audience. Because of his near blindness, he could not clearly see the appreciative crowd, but he could tell by the applause that he had finally composed another hit. The Irish tour was ultimately a huge success, and news quickly reached England that the composer had made a mighty comeback.

A few months later Handel took his newest work to the London stage. Everyone who was anyone found a way into the concert hall for the first few performances. On the second night King George II was so moved by the Messiah's message that the monarch stood when he heard the "Hallelujah Chorus." When the audience saw the king standing, they followed suit. Thus, a tradition was born that called for all to rise during the performance of this song. The custom would continue throughout the rest of Handel's life and even to this day. With his vision so dimmed, the master composer could not see the awe this chorus inspired in his listeners, but he must have been able to feel it.

Handel's annual Eastertide performances to benefit his favorite charity, the Foundling Hospital, kept the Messiah's composer out of debtors' prison and in the public eye for another seventeen years. He conducted his most beloved work a final time just eight days before his death in 1759. A portion of it was even played at his funeral, after which he was buried with honors at Westminster Abbey. Yet as great as the response to the *Messiah* had been during his life, its popularity began to fade after Handel's death. Soon people hardly ever heard even a portion of the oratorio at Easter. Amazingly, by the 1770s the great *Messiah* was viewed as an old-fashioned piece of music whose time had come and gone.

In 1788 another legendary composer, Wolfgang Amadeus Mozart, took a stab at updating Handel's oratorio. In performances given in Vienna during the spring of 1789, Mozart expanded the original concept of the *Messiah* to include a full orchestra and more singers. He also cut the production and updated the arrangements, even changing melodies and harmonies to better fit with popular music of the time. Mozart's magic failed to make Handel's work more popular, and the new version, while not dismissed, did not become a rage in either Europe or England. It might have been forgotten altogether if not for a revival of oratorios during the English music festivals of the 1820s.

Performed largely by amateur music lovers and sometimes crude in nature, it was through these music festivals that the common people were finally able to hear Handel's work. A host of Handel's pieces were performed, but of his many oratorios, the *Messiah* quickly became the favorite. In less than a decade Handel's last great work became an essential part of almost every music festival, in small towns and large cities. It even became common for parts of the oratorio to be taught to schoolchildren and sung in Sunday school classes.

The upper class caught wind of Handel's oratorio's new fame and demanded that it be played at the major concert halls as well. In the Victorian tradition, this led to grand, new productions featuring choirs of over one thousand singers. It also led Sir George Grove—a onetime civil engineer and songwriter whose talents as the latter would lead to his being named director of the Royal College of Music—to restore the oratorio to its original form. He cut out Mozart's changes and directed the piece just as Handel had. In its original form, the oratorio became an Easter favorite of young and old, rich and poor, Protestant and Catholic. It was deemed the perfect musical presentation for the time when Christians remembered Christ's death and resurrection.

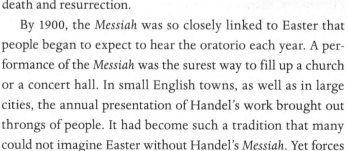

By 1900, the *Messiah* was so closely linked to Easter that people began to expect to hear the oratorio each year. A performance of the *Messiah* was the surest way to fill up a church or a concert hall. In small English towns, as well as in large cities, the annual presentation of Handel's work brought out throngs of people. It had become such a tradition that many could not imagine Easter without Handel's *Messiah*. Yet forces were at work that would shift the oratorio's popularity to a completely different time of the year and, in a sense, change its impact as well.

The *Messiah's* move to Christmas was based more on marketing than on anyone's suddenly realizing that the "Hallelujah Chorus" and other parts of the oratorio would magnify the significance of the celebration of Christ's birth. The large crowds that turned out each Easter to hear the oratorio prompted marketers to rethink the timing of the annual presentation of Handel's work. Those raising money for charities knew that people's spirit of giving was far greater at Christmas than at Easter. Another knock against Easter was its very short holiday season, which lasted only three days. Meanwhile, by the time of World War II Christmas had grown into a holiday that stretched for at least three weeks in Britain and Europe and as long as a month in the United States. Thus, to those needing to raise money for charities, the Christmas season seemed the perfect time to showcase the *Messiah*. Not only could Handel's masterpiece be performed for weeks instead of only a weekend, but with so many caught up in a wave of generosity, more money could be raised too. With fund raising as the driving force, the Messiah began to be performed during December as well as during the Easter weekend. It was an immediate Christmas hit.

For some years, Handel's oratorio was part of both the Christmas and Easter holiday experiences, especially in England. But by the 1960s, the *Messiah* had been almost completely transformed into a Christmas event. With community and college choirs joining the long list of churches and theaters that annually performed the oratorio, it became more popular than ever before.

Today Handel's most revered work remains the best-known and most-loved classical vocal piece in the world. It is now almost always thought of as a Christmas musical. Handel probably would have been shocked, but not disappointed, by this change of seasons.

Charles Burney, an eighteenth-century music historian, remarked that Handel's oratorio "fed the hungry, clothed the naked, and fostered the orphan." As a presentation that has raised millions of dollars for charity, the *Messiah* has done all that and more. It has also dramatically raised spiritual awareness for millions of people.

Respected music historian Robert Manson Myers gave a glimpse of the power of the *Messiah* when he wrote, "For the first time in musical history the mighty drama of human redemption was treated as an epic poem." Yet it was more than this; the oratorio was so inspired that the Bible story comes to life for almost all who hear it performed. It does more than arouse the intellect; it takes root in the soul.

Another music historian, R. A. Streatfield, saw the *Messiah* as "the first instance in the history of music of an attempt to view the mighty drama of human redemption from an artistic viewpoint." It might not have been the first, but none before or since has done it better.

Inspired by the letter of a friend and prompted to action by mounting debts, George Handel birthed a piece of music that touches the heart and mind, bringing almost all who hear it closer to an understanding of God's grand plan, which began with the creation of the earth and was magnified beyond comprehension by the birth of a child in a manger. Handel's *Messiah* is the story of life and death, resurrection and redemption, pain and glory, and hope beyond all measure.

In the three weeks that he composed his greatest work, Handel sensed that the *Messiah* was different from anything else he had ever written. He later told friends that when he contemplated each act, "I did think I did see all Heaven before me and the great God himself." It would have taken that kind of inspiration to create a work so powerful that one small segment of that work, the "Hallelujah Chorus," still brings people to their feet and leads people to the Lord. We will never know the incredible emotions experienced by Mary, Joseph, the shepherds, and the wise men when they first saw Jesus, but through Handel's *Messiah* we can sense a bit of the awesome power and glory that illuminated the first Christmas and that continues to magnify the birth of Jesus today.

15

HOLLY

Holly can be found in almost all of the decorating schemes used during the Christmas holidays. Associated with Christmas for almost seventeen hundred years, holly was also an important facet of December life hundreds of years before Christ was born. This shiny plant has a unique power for many believers—not magical power, but symbolic power.

Though early Christians were familiar with the use of holly thanks to the Romans' use of it during winter solstice festivals, holly's initial significance probably began with the Celts. Many people who maintained a close tie with nature considered the plant one of the two most important plants in the woods. Holly's earliest significance was established by one of history's most mysterious groups, the Druids.

Today the Druids are primarily remembered as being wizards, but they were much more. In the ancient Celtic society of England, they were the judges, educators, historians, doctors, astronomers, and astrologers. Roman history shows they were filling these roles as early as two hundred years before Christ.

In fact, the Druids probably had been plying these trades for centuries before that.

Trees and plants were very important in Celtic mythology. The Druids believed a constant war was going on between the "Oak King" and the "Holly King." These "twins" both wanted to control the forest. Holly always won in the winter as the oaks lost their leaves and stood bare before the evergreen plant. In this season, holly caught everyone's attention.

Because of the "magical" power of the holly to survive and prosper in even the darkest and cruelest winters, Druids instructed the Celts that this plant was the most powerful plant in the woods. Thus, people picked boughs of holly and brought them into their homes. They believed the tree's magic would help protect them from the evil they believed infused the season of night. They also thought that holly, the plant that could tame the bitter wind, had the power to bring peace and understanding. So during disputes, angry parties would stand under holly trees to work out their differences.

Roman soldiers probably brought the concept of decorating with holly back to their country when they returned from duty in Britain. The shiny plant quickly took on a life of its own in the civilized world. Because it grew in winter, it quickly became associated with the winter solstice and with one of the most important gods in Roman mythology.

During December, when the Romans marked the shortest days of the year with a weeklong festival honoring Saturn, holly wreaths with bright red berries were given as gifts.

During this week of wild celebration and partying, holly could be seen inside and outside homes, on streets, in public buildings, and in shops. It was sold, swapped, and given as a gift. Wreaths were woven with images of Saturn hanging from the boughs or positioned in the center of the arrangement.

Romans believed, much like the Celts, that holly had the power to bring good luck. Hence, the more holly you had in your home, the luckier you would be. The people of Rome also felt that the plant warded off lightning strikes; a home containing holly would better survive a storm than one that was undecorated and therefore unprotected. Holly was also thought to drive away the evil powers of black magic. During this superstitious era, any plant that would keep witches at bay was considered invaluable.

Savvy merchants, sensing an opportunity to enhance profits, continued to expand the uses of the plant. The sellers of the holly even convinced some that touching it would cure a host of diseases. It seemed that the more money the plant generated, the more powerful it became to the Roman people.

In the first and second centuries, a time when many Romans began to convert to Christianity, the persecution of believers drove worship underground. In a society that made a sport of killing Christians, believers had to be very careful in order to remain safe. Thus, even the most devout followers of Jesus decked their homes with holly during the Saturnalia festival. Over the next two hundred years, a time when Christianity would emerge as the state religion, Christian and pagan Romans alike had problems recalling the origins of certain annual customs. Holly was one of the old Roman holiday traditions adopted or absorbed by Christians. But as it became a symbol of Christian faith, its meaning changed.

Christians began using holly as a teaching tool to explain the life and death of Christ. Initially the prickly leaves represented the crown of thorns that had been placed on Jesus' head on the day of the crucifixion. The plant's red berries were to remind believers of the blood that the Savior shed on the cross for their sins. This association between the crucifixion and holly quickly spread, and as it did, legends and stories about this link abounded.

Thanks to the Christian symbolism passed on by a host of early church missionaries and clerics, in Germany holly was called *Christdorn*. According to a German legend, it was actually holly branches that had been woven into the painful crown that was placed on Christ's head while the soldiers mocked him saying, "Hail, King of the Jews." The Germans also taught that holly berries had been white until the crown of thorns cut into Jesus' brow. His blood was so powerful that it not only turned the berries on his crown to crimson, but every holly berry in the entire world suddenly turned red.

Another legend soon evolved about the holly tree. This legend claimed that the wood of a holly tree was used to construct the cross. It was said that none of the trees in the woods would bow to the axe of those constructing the cross. Each time a man hit a tree with the sharp blade, the tree would explode into cinder-sized fragments rather than give itself to this evil purpose. When the holly tree allowed itself to be chopped down and formed into a cross, it became known as the chosen tree and was therefore given the position of being the tree that was part of God's grand plan of redemption. As such, it became a symbol of the passion.

Yet another legend associated with holly is much like a legend attributed to another Christmas plant, the poinsettia. In this story, an orphan boy who had been adopted by the shepherds was in the field with them when the angels appeared to announce the birth of Jesus. The child traveled with the men to see the babe in the manger. When he arrived, he was not only deeply moved but also embarrassed; he had no gift to present to the baby. The poor little boy resorted to the only skill he really knew and wove a crown for this newborn king. He chose limbs from a holly tree as the material for the project. When he laid the modest gift on the baby's head, Jesus touched the crown and it began to sparkle. The orphan was so deeply affected that he cried, his tears falling on the holly. When the child's tears touched the plant's white berries, it turned them a beautiful, deep scarlet. Some people believe that this legend was part of the inspiration behind the Christmas carol "Little Drummer

Boy." There is no proof of this, but the legend, coupled with the already existing use of holly by the Romans in December, probably did pave the way for holly's being more closely associated with Christ's birth than his death.

A final story that fully illustrates the plant's firm link to Christian history and tradition is found, not in the history and lore of the green plant itself, but in its name. Because of holly's association with the crucifixion, some scholars believe that the word "holy" was extracted from the word "holly." There is nothing to definitively link the two words, but if this is true, the plant is likely behind the word "holiday" and is therefore tied to Christmas in another unique fashion.

A host of songs and poems have been written about this plant so steeped in ancient lore. The fact that it has its roots in pagan rituals should not deter Christians from using holly as one of the Christmas season's most profound symbols. While a majority of Christmas traditions deal strictly with the birth of Christ or with secular legends, holly stands apart, reminding us what the Christ child was sent here to do. Thus, once thought powerful because it could survive even the toughest winter, holly has become a symbol of the strength that is available to all who call upon the name of the Lord.

16

LIGHTS

Martin Luther transformed the look of the Christmas tree forever after a late-night December walk through the German woods almost five hundred years ago. Enthralled with the way the starlight looked as it filtered through branches of evergreen trees, he felt as if the hand of God had touched his soul and had allowed him to see the world in a much different way. Stopping on a snow-covered rise, he studied the scene for some time. Its tranquil beauty and soft light brought a great sense of peace to Luther.

Determined to duplicate the atmosphere of that outdoor scene inside his own home, the minister attached candleholders to the tree's limbs and wowed his family and friends with the first brightly lit Christmas tree. From this humble beginning, the custom of putting candles on Christmas trees quickly swept across Germany.

Because of the new interest in lighting Christmas trees, craftsmen began to produce ornate candleholders that were made just for using on tree limbs. Specially designed and multicolored candles soon followed. By the mid-1800s, a beautiful fir tree, trimmed with ornaments and lit by scores of candles, came to represent two things. First, it came to represent the perfect Christmas scene. It was pictured over and over again by illustrations in magazines, newspapers, books, and on Christmas cards. In just three centuries, the lighted Christmas tree had evolved into as much a symbol of the season as had St. Nicholas and the nativity scene.

But the Christmas tree also came to represent an extremely dangerous fire hazard. Countless trees were set ablaze by candles, thousands of homes were burned to the ground annually when a candle ignited a tree limb, and hundreds of people died each year in fires started by Christmas-tree candles. Yet the beautiful glow of the candlelight, even if it was a major fire risk, meant so much to so many people that concerned firemen could not convince even their own families to give up using these fiery decorations. It would take both time and technology to blow out the Christmas-tree candles.

In 1879 Thomas Edison changed the way America illuminated houses, with his invention of the lightbulb. Three years later, one of his employees, Edward Johnson, decided to apply this new invention to the Christmas tree.

As had become their family custom, in 1882 the Johnsons purchased an evergreen tree and put it up in the parlor of the family's New York home. As they decorated the newly cut tree, Johnson was struck with an idea. Using the process of the Edison laboratories, Johnson produced a string of eighty small and brightly colored electric lightbulbs. Much brighter than the light of a similar number of candles, the bulbs gave off a constant glow that was almost intoxicating. Johnson took them home and strung them around his tree. As the lights lit up the room and shone through a large window, neighbors began to walk by the house and marvel at what they saw. As most people did not even have electricity, the sight of a green tree illuminated by lightbulbs seemed almost magical. Yet even more incredible was that Johnson's lights didn't just glow; they flashed off and on.

Even in a city the size of New York, the Edison employee's inventive decorations created a great stir. A parade of people constantly walked by the Johnsons' home, and scores of people knocked on the front door, asking to see the tree up close. A reporter visiting from Michigan was even assigned to cover the story for the Detroit Post and Tribune.

Last evening I walked over beyond Fifth Avenue and called at the residence of Edward H. Johnson, vice-president of Edison's electric company. There, at the rear of the beautiful parlors, was a large Christmas tree presenting a most picturesque and uncanny aspect. It was brilliantly lighted with many colored globes about as large as an English walnut and was turning some six times a minute on a little pine box. There were eighty lights in all encased in these dainty glass eggs, and about equally divided between white, red and blue. As the tree turned, the colors alternated, all the lamps going out and being relit at every revolution. The result was a continuous twinkling of dancing colors, red, white, blue, white, red, blue, all evening.

I need not tell you that the scintillating evergreen was a pretty sight—one can hardly imagine anything prettier. The ceiling was crossed obliquely with two wires on which hung 28 more of the tiny lights; and all the lights and the fantastic tree itself with its starry fruit were kept going by the slight electric current brought from the main office on a filmy wire. The tree was kept revolving by a little hidden crank below the floor which was turned by electricity. It was a superb exhibition.

The *Detroit Post and Tribune* was just the first of many newspapers to call at the Johnson home. Yet even though the tree made news across the country, Edison did not jump on the bandwagon and create Christmas lights for commercial sale. That would have been putting the cart before the horse, as most Americans would not have electric power in their homes for years.

In 1908 Ralph Morris, who had never heard of Edward Johnson and his Christmas lights, began to consider how to make Christmas a safer holiday for his family. His small son had recently dropped a candle onto one of the limbs of the family tree, causing a minor fire and slightly injuring the boy. To eliminate the use of candles in his home, Johnson purchased an old telephone switchboard, yanked off the wiring and lights, and strung them around the tree. For many years, Morris's family and friends believed that he had invented Christmas-tree lights. While Morris had created the first lights to grace a middle-class home, scores of wealthy families in New York, Boston, and Washington, D.C., had been throwing Christmas-light parties for more than a decade.

In the years between Johnson's twinkling Christmas tree and Morris's solution to the fire hazard of candles, several companies investigated the possibility of producing electric Christmas lights. The stumbling block was always the expense. A string of bulbs like the one Johnson had created for his tree cost over $100 in materials alone. Many Americans didn't make that much money in a year. Also, as screw-in sockets had yet to be invented, each bulb would have to be wired individually. When the bulbs burned out or were broken, an electrician would have to be called to replace them. But even in the face of these problems, Edison and others worked to convince at least the wealthy that Christmas lights were the best way to illuminate the holiday season.

One of the first converts to electric Christmas lights was President Grover Cleveland. In 1895 the president was ecstatic to claim the first tree in Washington to be lit by electric lights. The huge evergreen sported more than one hundred red, blue, and green bulbs and was the talk of the town, which created a buying frenzy among the nation's elite. If the White House had electric lights, then the country-club group had to have them too.

Within five years, many members of the social set in New York had spent as much as $3000 per tree to outlight their neighbor's evergreen. At country estates, where there were no power lines, the rich purchased generators and hired electricians full-time just to keep the Christmas lights burning. But Edison, while excited by the new holiday use of his invention, knew there would never be any profits in Christmas lights until they could be manufactured cheaply and sold to the masses.

By 1910, General Electric had introduced a string of eight lights that could be purchased for $12. The price was far beyond the reach of most consumers, so the lights were used mostly in store displays. Two years later, Ever Ready, the company that would become famous for batteries, introduced a slightly cheaper set to the market. Some upper-middle-class consumers purchased a few sets, but most Americans had to continue using candles.

Outdoor light displays in Boston and New York City began to grab the public's interest in the days just before World War I. As improvements in manufacturing and bulb quality lowered production costs, several other companies jumped on board. After the war, when prices had dropped low enough for Christmas lights to be offered in stores where the middle class shopped, electric holiday light sales finally took off. The market for Christmas lights would continue to grow rapidly until the next world war.

In 1924 General Electric and Westinghouse introduced a new set of Christmas lights that would become the industry standard for the next fifty years. These multicolored long-lasting bulbs burned cooler and offered better lighting than ever before. Best of all, they were so inexpensive that almost everyone could afford to buy a set. When electrical power lines began to reach even the most rural parts of the nation, the average American Christmas quickly became a festival of electric lights.

The years after World War II brought the advent of lighted ornaments, bubble lights, lighted snowflakes and icicles, and even lighted Santas, and the lighting of Christmas gave each family a chance to individualize the look and color of their tree. Christmas lights also helped Christmas to move out of the parlor and into people's yards.

The tradition of the national Christmas-tree-lighting ceremony on the White House lawn was started in 1923 by President Calvin Coolidge. This tradition has continued ever since, interrupted only by the blackouts of World War II. In 1933 Rockefeller Center created another annual tradition with its huge lighted tree in New York City. All across the nation, communities strung lights on trees, on buildings, and across streets. Most cities even invested in lighted street decorations that hung from lampposts and utility poles. Today billions of lights are used each holiday season by municipalities alone. Tens of billions more lights can be found in private homes.

Almost five centuries ago, Martin Luther taught his children that the candles that burned on the Christmas tree stood for the light that Jesus brought into the world. As time went by, a candle on a tree came to represent a prayer that needed to be answered or a loved one who had departed from this world. As electricity changed the way trees were lit and expanded the use of lights at Christmas, the simple meaning of what Luther first observed in the starlit woods was obscured and replaced by an often blinding glow of millions of tiny bulbs that turns night into day. Yet the glow that drew people to Martin Luther's and Edward Johnson's trees still beckons people of all ages today.

Two thousands years ago, Christ was born into a dark world that would be dramatically changed by his life and his death. When he rose from the dead and ascended back to heaven, he left the earth a much brighter place. In a very real sense, the glow of billions of electric Christmas lights reinforces just how deeply the babe in the manger has changed and is still changing the world. Martin Luther would have liked that.

17

MISTLETOE

It might seem strange to many people that each Christmas season, mistletoe—a parasitic plant—has the unique, mischievous, and delightful role of holiday matchmaker. Yet a stolen kiss on a cold moonlit evening is only one of many reasons that for centuries this waxy, green-leafed plant has been tacked over doorways all around the world during the month of December.

The plant received its name from second-century Anglo-Saxons. In Old English, *mistel* is the word for "dung," and *tan* means "twig." *Misteltan* is the Old-English version of the word we know today as mistletoe. The name implies that the plant sprang to life from bird droppings on tree branches. The inspiration behind the plant's christening, though true, might seem a bit crude and distasteful today, but to the people of the first and second century it was a radiant sign of God's power to bring life from death, to create something beautiful and robust from something ugly and useless.

In ancient times, mistletoe was viewed with awe. It was considered a miracle plant. During the harshest days of winter's fury, when most everything else had died, this small, flowering, seemingly rootless plant thrived in the treetops. It offered beauty and color, life and hope, mystery and wonder.

Even before the time of Christ, the early Greeks and Celts believed mistletoe was sacred. They taught that only God's powerful touch could bring a new plant out of winter's deadwood and nourish that plant during the year's most brutal days. For this reason, people of many different faiths have considered mistletoe a sacred and noble gift that represents life, hope, and security. Many Christians even believed it was the key to understanding God and his purpose for humankind. They claimed that if you understood how mistletoe grew, why it survived and thrived each winter season, as well as how it spread, you would understand the Lord and your relationship with him.

It seems strange that a parasite, a plant that literally sucks the life out of another living organism, could inspire such awe. Yet mistletoe is radically different from most of nature's other parasites. It is a beautiful, flowing plant that flourishes at a time when all other living creatures fight for life. Its growth cannot be controlled, nor, it seems, can the plant be eradicated. It seems to grow out of nothing and yet appears to be everywhere. It is little wonder that ancient civilizations were so mystified by mistletoe.

Scandinavian warriors would stop fierce battles if they or the opposing soldiers suddenly found themselves under trees where mistletoe grew. They believed that to continue a war beneath the plant that God had given the world as a sign of life would dishonor him. A host of other societies soon adopted this rule as well. For millions of people, mistletoe became not just a symbol of peace, but a sign that demanded peace.

Growing out of its role as peacemaker, mistletoe took on another role—that of protector. Plants were cut from trees and nailed or tied over the doors of homes and barns to ward off enemies. Mistletoe was said to be so powerful that even the most fearsome of the forest's beasts would not threaten a home with the plant hung on its door.

By the Middle Ages, mistletoe was placed over babies' cribs to ward off illness and evil spirits. Mistletoe's leaves and berries, though poisonous if ingested raw, were diluted and used in medicines. The plant was credited with treating epilepsy, apoplexy, palsy, tuberculosis, and stroke. Even today mistletoe is being studied by researchers as an antidote in the fight against cancer. Yet while mistletoe could heal if used in the right way, it was supposedly the ultimate weapon when used in a negative way.

A Norse legend held that mistletoe shaped into an arrow was the most powerful force in the world and could instantly bring down the mightiest warrior. The only way this fallen soldier could be saved was if a loved one used mistletoe berries to restore his life.

As this legend of the restorative power of mistletoe berries migrated to England, the plant became a symbol of love. When a couple passed under the plant, they had to stop and kiss. If they did, God would bless them with everlasting love. Still, to make sure that this custom was not abused, the boy had to pick one berry for each kiss. When the berries were gone, the kissing was supposed to end.

Charles Dickens even wrote about mistletoe in one of his epics. The great writer's words in *A Christmas Carol* emphasized the strange power the plant held over those who encountered it. "From the centre of the ceiling of this kitchen, old Wardle had just suspended with his own hands a huge branch of mistletoe, and this same branch of mistletoe instantaneously gave rise to a scene of general and most delightful struggling and confusion; in the midst of which, Mr. Pickwick, with a gallantry that would have done honour to a descendant of Lady Tollimglower herself, took the old lady by the hand, led her beneath the mystic branch, and saluted her in all courtesy and decorum."

At about the time that Dickens wrote this, in 1843, Christians adopted mistletoe as a Christmas symbol. The English Christians knew that Christ had brought the promise of everlasting life to a barren and hopeless world. When Christ's message was beginning to shake the very core of the world, the leaders in power decided to nail him to a tree. They believed this would end Christ's influence and halt his message. But like the mistletoe, the beauty and power of the Son of God sprang forth from the tree on which he was nailed, and the world took note. For Christians, the plant thus became a symbol of life after death, of faith that was so strong it could grow even in the midst of the darkness. Like mistletoe, God's love and true faith could survive even the most barbarous times and the darkest days. And believing in Jesus as Savior brought personal peace even in the midst of war.

Christians across Europe seized upon the religious symbolism of mistletoe and no longer posted the plant over their doors to ward off evil spirits but to show the world that they believed in the love God had sent the world through his Son, Jesus Christ. The power of the plant that thrived in the toughest of times also represented their faith. Christians believed that God would see them through persecution, wars, famines, and plagues. His grace would cover them even on the darkest, coldest days.

A French legend further enhanced the view of mistletoe as a sign of God's love and further endeared the plant to Christians everywhere. The legend stated that a single sprig of mistletoe grew on the cross where Jesus died. It was said that the plant represented the undying love God had revealed to the world through the sacrifice of his Son and the new life that would spring from the brutality that had taken place on the cross. The roots of this new growth would not be visible but would be nourished by something unseen. Thus, mistletoe not only symbolized faith; it also came to stand for a love that would not die. As mistletoe crossed the world from tree to tree, so the story of Jesus—his life, death, and resurrection—crossed the world from person to person. And though many powerful men tried to halt and discredit that message, they had no more success than those who had tried to rid the natural world of mistletoe.

For hundreds of years, people of faith who kissed under mistletoe vowed to keep not only their love for each other strong but their love for the Lord as well. Along with the faith and love represented by the plant that grew strong even in the harshest days of winter came a hope and understanding that brought peace to all who truly believed. Through their faith, the Christians of the time proved the ancient Greeks' and Celts' prophecy correct: mistletoe did indeed hold a key to understanding God's greatest and most important gift to the world.

Today the mistletoe's Christian message of peace, faith, and hope has been largely lost, but even if in a rather childish fashion, the message of love has remained. That is why mistletoe is mentioned in countless Christmas songs, movies, and TV shows. The green-and-red plant can be seen topping silly hats and decorating all kinds of clothing. It can also still be found hanging over millions of doors.

In a world that often embraces Christmas without embracing its real meaning, maybe it is time to bring mistletoe back into the church. Maybe by having the green sprig with red berries hanging in a house of worship, people can reclaim mistletoe as the symbol of sustaining faith, hope, and love.

~ 18 ~
MOVIES OF CHRISTMAS

Over the past ninety years, hundreds of movies have embraced Christmas. These films have employed every motion-picture genre, from musicals to family dramas, from war movies to horror flicks, from comedy to fantasy. They have included classics such as *It's a Wonderful Life* and forgettable, low-budget bombs like *Santa Claus vs. the Martians*. Yet of the hundreds of films churned out by the show-business machine, only a few have been so loved that watching them has become a holiday tradition in the United States and around the world. Surely the reason these select films have become such an important Christmas tradition for millions of people can be traced to the films' messages of hope, faith, redemption, honesty, and joy.

None of the traditional holiday classics actually centers on the real story of the first Christmas. Yet while Hollywood has not chosen to make a film centering on the birth of Jesus, it has used the message of that event and the example of Christ's life in abstract ways to embrace themes that are vital to living a Christian life. In fact, the movies that have become holiday classics are really morality plays and are wonderful tools for teaching the importance of the most noble of human qualities, which are perhaps the greatest gifts to be shared during this special season.

Charles Dickens's wonderful book *A Christmas Carol* has been made into films many times, with a wide variety of new names and settings. Movie historians have long argued over which version is the greatest, but there are now more than a dozen versions that ring true to the book and its lessons, and new versions will probably be made in the future. It seems that the world never tires of this classic story.

Hollywood first brought this classic to the screen in 1938. Reginald Owen played Scrooge, and the great character actor Gene Lockhart filled the role of his faithful employee. True to the original book, this American film was set in England during a Victorian Christmas and represented the Hollywood studio system at its very best. Yet many believe that the 1957 British version of *A Christmas Carol* was the first to fully define the story. Among the host of other wanna-bes that have been produced in the past forty years, two of the most popular versions of Dickens's classic are probably the 1970 musical Scrooge, starring Albert Finney, and *The Muppet Christmas Carol*, starring Kermit the Frog and all his colorful friends.

What makes each of these movies so outstanding is that they never stray far from the lessons of the importance of family and giving that were the theme of Dickens's book. As the novel was important in recasting Christmas as a holiday for families, especially children, the film depictions of *A Christmas Carol* are important reminders that beyond all the commercialization of the modern Christmas, the gathering of family and the joy of giving should remain the heart of every celebration.

No matter the setting, almost every version of *A Christmas Carol* embraces the story's British roots. But *Miracle on 34th Street* is uniquely American. This tale of a department-store Santa who seems to be the real Mr. Claus and a girl from a family too cynical to believe in such nonsense, *Miracle on 34th Street* is a movie that fully gives itself over to faith. Beautifully written and wonderfully acted, the 1947 version of Miracle, with Edmund Gwen, Maureen O'Hara, Natalie Wood, and Gene Lockhart, is the best Santa Claus movie ever made. This black-and-white version of the film has never been unseated or replaced by a host of color remakes because the movie truly captures the spirit of wishing for things unseen and having the faith to believe that somehow, some way, those dreams can come true. And like *A Christmas Carol*, this version of *Miracle on 34th* Street proves there is no place for cynicism at Christmastime. *Miracle* reinforces the belief that when all negative emotions are replaced by the joy and wonder of the season, anything can happen—even miracles.

One of the ironies of *Miracle on 34th Street* is that it was released in the summer and was not advertised as a Christmas film. The studio had no faith in Christmas or in the movie. But as crowds flocked to theaters to catch the film in the midst of the long, hot days of July, and as the picture was still playing in movie houses six months later during the cold holiday season's evenings, Hollywood learned its lesson. Christmas movies would work. The success of this film thus paved the way for studios to make more projects centered on holiday themes.

Though not a critical success at the time of its release, *White Christmas* now ranks as one of the most beloved films of all time. The picture was made to capitalize on the popularity of Bing Crosby's version of Irving Berlin's classic Christmas song, "White Christmas." The best-selling Christmas song of all time, this song made its debut in the 1942 hit movie *Holiday Inn*. Yet in that film, the song and Christmas Day were just a small part of the movie. The impact of both, however, were significant enough that a dozen years later Hollywood opted to have Berlin score a new musical around the song and Christmas. With a story line that brought a group of World War II veterans together to honor the general who had led them through the toughest battles of their lives, *White Christmas* was a box-office smash and remains a favorite today. The music in this film probably drives its popularity, but the images of men paying tribute to someone who gave so much for them still tugs at the heart strings as it teaches wonderful lessons about respect and love.

Christmas in Connecticut, released in 1945, presents the precept of how love can grow only in a climate of honesty. A love story that can been enjoyed by the whole family, in this romantic comedy Dennis Morgan falls for Barbara Stanwyck with the help of a wide array of great character actors including Sidney Greenstreet and S. Z. Sakall. This movie projects the holiday ideal of love and family in a unique and refreshing fashion. It is an old Hollywood screwball comedy, perhaps too innocent, sweet, and predictable for jaded viewers, but for those who really believe in the joys of love and who want to be submerged in the magical Christmas atmosphere, this film is perfect. They don't make movies like this anymore, and it's a real shame.

As great as these first four movies are, it seems that almost everyone's favorite Christmas movie is *It's a Wonderful Life*. The story is well known. A man, George, who has sacrificed all of his dreams for his family and friends, suddenly loses everything. When his world comes apart during the holidays, he senses that his life has been wasted. Caught in a deep depression, George feels he has done nothing to change the world and decides to take his own life. But a bumbling angel named Clarence comes to his rescue. Clarence shows George the profound impact he's had on hundreds of people in his town and around the world. This movie ends with many of the people whom George has touched giving him the money to save his business. This proves to George that his life has been worthwhile, and it earns Clarence his wings.

When this Capra film was released in 1946, many felt that the film's moral lessons were presented in a much too heavy-handed manner. Some believed that James Stewart's acting was over the top, Donna Reed's portrayal of the wife was too perfect, and the ending of the story was too ideal. Yet in retrospect, the critics were wrong, and the story of how *It's a Wonderful Life* grew to become a beloved classic is a mirror image of the moral taught in the movie. Though nominated for several Academy Awards, the film was quickly dismissed by movie patrons when it was released. At the time, movie fans were drawn to gritty, realistic dramas that rarely included fairy-tale endings. *It's a Wonderful Life* was completely out of step with the times. Like its lead character, the film seemed doomed to make little impact on the world. But unlike George, the movie didn't seem to have a guardian angel until TV became the American family's primary entertainment focus.

With the advent of television, *It's a Wonderful Life* received a second chance. People were trying to make sense of the Cold War and Vietnam and found a great deal of satisfaction in the message of an angel looking out for someone who was just trying to do his everyday job. More important was the film's most powerful lesson: even the most menial life can make a powerful impact on society.

Families, churches, and even some journalists drew on the precepts found in *It's a Wonderful Life* to show that a single life could influence the course of world events. The movie's lead character was the embodiment of the rewards earned by putting faith, sacrifice, truth, loyalty, and honor into action. Thus, while the film contained a message easy to embrace at Christmas, it was also a message that could and should be lived every day, which is probably why the film's popularity grows with each passing holiday season.

The five films covered here are probably the most popular Christmas classics, yet a host of others, including Bob Hope's *The Lemon-Drop Kid*, Cary Grant's *The Bishop's Wife*, Gary Cooper's *Meet John Doe*, Janet Leigh's *Holiday Affair*, Darren McGavin's *A Christmas Story*, and Irene Dunn's *Penny Serenade*, are also films that depict life lessons that enhance the values of the Christmas season. Like *It's a Wonderful Life*, *White Christmas*, *A Christmas Carol*, *Christmas in Connecticut*, and *Miracle on 34th Street*, these movies bring families together, shed light on the importance of selfless giving, love, and charity, while emphasizing the joy and wonder of the season. Thus, in a media-oriented world, they are a very important part of a modern holiday celebration.

With the success of all these great films, it seems strange that Hollywood has ignored the passion, power, and glory of the first Christmas. There are no great movies centering on the manger. There are no annually aired films that embrace the true Christmas story. This may well be a good thing, as Hollywood probably does a much better job of dealing with themes such as redemption and forgiveness in a symbolic fashion. Perhaps even Hollywood long ago realized that there is no way to capture the beauty and majesty of Christ's incarnation. The great screen directors have probably always known that even a multimillion-dollar budget and the world's greatest actors could not bring Jesus' birth to life nearly as well as the children in Christmas pageants who annually act out the story found in the Gospels of Luke and Matthew.

～ 19 ～
NATIVITY SCENES AND
CHRISTMAS PAGEANTS

There are two distinct images that define the life of Christ for most Christians and non-Christians alike: the cross and the manger. The cross is a haunting and stark picture. Many don't even like to try to imagine Jesus nailed to this instrument of torture and execution. So while the image of Christ on the cross is familiar, it does not bring joy or peace. Knowing that any person, especially the Son of God, died in such a way is very disturbing to most people.

In contrast, images of Christ's first days in the manger in Bethlehem usually conjure up joy, peace, and wonder. These scenes are almost always clear and beautiful in the minds of old and young alike. Remarkably, these pastoral images have been imprinted into hundreds of millions of minds, not so much through Scriptures, sermons, paintings, or even Hollywood films, as through observing simple nativity displays. These usually static displays have brought the first Christmas to life like nothing else ever has.

Luke 2:7 states that when Jesus was born, Mary laid him in a manger. The family had been forced to stay in what was probably a barn because all the inns in the town of Bethlehem were full due to the influx of people reporting for the census ordered by the Roman leader Caesar Augustus.

If a classic descriptive author such as John Steinbeck had written an account of the events in Bethlehem, the picture would have been filled with as much detail as a Norman Rockwell painting. But no description of that manger scene is found anywhere in the Bible. Nowhere does it say what animals, if any, were being kept there at the time. As the community was filled with visitors, it would seem logical that the stables would have been as full as the inns were. Yet nowhere is that fact recorded.

In Luke 2:16, it is clear that the shepherds traveled to the manger to see Jesus. Yet the Magi did not arrive in time to visit Jesus in his birthplace, nor, evidently, did they meet the shepherds. In Matthew 2:11, the writer points out that the wise men from the East were invited into the house where Mary and Joseph were staying. Once again the biblical scribes do not identify the location of this house or describe it at all. To the Gospel authors, none of these details were important.

In the Dark Ages in Eastern Europe, a few artists carved nativity pieces for display in homes and churches. These nativity carvings were some of the first Christmas decorations. Yet it wasn't until 1223 that a famous church leader brought the manger scene alive in the way many still experience it today. Though no one knows how long it took or what materials were used, St. Francis of Assisi constructed a nativity scene outside his church in Italy. Francis probably used wood for most of his initial display, though some historians believe he might have also employed local sculptors working in clay or stone. By today's standards, this nativity was assuredly crude, but since the creator was a cleric, it was undoubtedly biblically accurate. So while he probably used real people to play the principles and included the shepherds, it is unlikely that Francis would have added the wise men or even animals to his scene.

Francis's three-dimensional display may have been simple, but the priest did not allow the exhibit to be static. He envisioned his creation as a teaching tool, so rather than just put it together for people to look at it, Francis brought the Nativity alive and allowed children to view the display from the inside out and to sing songs that reflected the spirit of this special event in history.

Each year these local plays grew larger and more complex. Soon they took on a life of their own and created such a stir that people traveled many miles to hear the music and see the priest's depiction of Jesus' birthplace. The nativity plays eventually featured drama and rehearsed music. No longer were the shepherds just standing around; they arrived as if they were following a star. The other participants also acted, taking on their parts with a sincere passion that was rarely seen in this era. Best of all, people were deeply moved by these ancient versions of our modern Christmas pageants.

Nativity plays became so popular that they spread throughout Europe. By the Middle Ages, churches in France, Spain, and Germany were putting together nativity scenes and bringing them to life with drama and songs. By the 1700s, shops throughout Europe were selling tabletop nativity scenes. Because these scenes were created by artists rather than by the clergy, the wise men often joined the shepherds around the manger.

When Victorian Christmases took hold in the United States and England in the mid-nineteenth century, almost all churches finally opened their doors for Christmas Eve services. As carols were brought into the sanctuary, the outdoor nativity plays begun by St. Francis were soon adapted for worship services. While the songs often varied from church to church, as did the way the performances were staged, the one thing that almost always remained constant in the pageants was the pomp and ceremony associated with the arrival of the shepherds and the Magi. The children playing these parts, outfitted in first-century costumes, often captured the drama and majesty of the first Christmas better than any sermon or Sunday school lesson ever could.

As Christmas pageants grew in popularity, they expanded into schools and theaters. By the early 1900s, many groups were presenting these Christmas plays in outdoor parks and theaters. As the presentations often ran for a week or more, the props were left on the set. Often as many visitors came by to view the sets during the daytime as to watch the play during the evening.

In some countries—such as Mexico, Germany, France, and Spain—cities began to take the nativity play to the streets. As in days of old, Mary and Joseph would search the city for a place to stay, then the shepherds and wise men would go house to house, trying to find Jesus. Often viewed in parade fashion as the events played out in neighborhoods and city squares, the action usually culminated at a full-size outdoor manger scene.

Following World War I, some churches and public buildings began to construct and display large, lighted manger scenes. This practice continued to grow in popularity, and by the 1950s, a number of businesses were selling manufactured nativity scenes to be used as yard decorations. Just as in the Dark Ages, when families often added a new hand-carved figure to their tiny tabletop nativity scenes each Christmas, many American families began to annually add to their outdoor nativity scene. With the introduction of lawn ornaments made of nonfading, longer-lasting materials, often intricate and elaborate nativity displays can now be seen on almost every block in American communities at Christmastime.

The creative use of animals by zoos made the nativity reenactment seem even more lifelike. City zoo managers began to realize that they could create a living nativity scene by using the kinds of animals that might have been in the barn, as well as those used by the shepherds and the wise men on their trips to Bethlehem. These lively displays, usually organized by volunteer zoo workers, put a whole new spin on the typical plastic or wooden exhibits. By the 1970s, churches and zoos were coming together to stage dynamic outdoor Christmas pageants that probably captured the look and feel of the first Christmas better than any nativity set ever produced.

Today, in an age when many people feel that Christ has been removed from so many aspects of Christmas, nativity scenes are more popular than ever. More and more churches are not only using the Nativity as the basis for their Christmas pageants but are moving things outdoors with nightly live nativity displays. Even in our information age, the drama of the first Christmas, whether it is depicted in a colorful yard scene, an elaborate living presentation, or an opulent church pageant, still causes millions to stop and remember the simple beauty and wonder of those ancient days in Bethlehem.

St. Francis of Assisi would be pleased that what he began eight centuries ago in a small European village is now a vital and moving part of the holiday season for hundreds of millions of people around the world. He, and the other men and women who kept the image of Jesus' birth at the forefront of Christmas through the years, probably would not even mind that the shepherds and the wise men arrive to honor Christ at about the same time. After all, as is clear in every nativity scene, the focus is never really on the visitors or the parents. The star is shining over Jesus.

～ 20 ～

THE NUTCRACKER BALLET

*The Nutcracke*r ballet is perhaps the most unique Christmas tradition. Considering that this ballet was adapted from a morbid story written for adults, brought to the theater by a famous composer who had great reservations about the project's merit and especially about its Christmas setting, and originally staged by students and opening to bad reviews, one would think the ballet would have been doomed to obscurity, lost in the maze of other failed holiday theatrical productions. But *The Nutcracker* survived, somehow hanging on to life in communist Russia until finally finding a magical platform in a place that rarely embraced classical culture—Cold War – era United States.

Could it have been a Christmas miracle that brought about the moment when the meshing of two enemies' cultures took *The Nutcracker* to the world? Or was it simply that the story was written in the universal language understood and embraced by children of all cultures—the language of fantasy, wonder, and joy—and all it needed was an international stage to bring that point home?

Dating back to the twelfth century, the nutcracker (the tool, not the ballet) was a facet of every household's annual holiday celebration. Nuts were a special treat saved for the Christmas season, and nutcrackers were used to extract the fruit from its hard shell. Children would sit around the winter's fire and wait for their fathers to carefully crack open nuts. Then the head of the household would share these delicacies, making sure each child received the same amount. Today this wouldn't seem like much of a Christmas treat for most children, but in the Middle Ages, nuts were morsels that kids looked forward to all year. Eating nuts was one of the most cherished customs of the season.

When Christmas trees began to appear in Germany, nuts were often used as decorations on the evergreens. The hard-shelled fruit was tied to the limbs, where it tempted children for weeks. When the tree was finally taken down, usually on the twelfth day of Christmas, fathers and mothers would bring out the nutcracker and share the goodies with their eager offspring. So even before becoming a holiday ballet, the nutcracker was an important element of the Christmas season. Perhaps that is why E. T. A. Hoffman chose the nutcracker as a part of the title for his dark story of magical dreams in 1816.

Hoffman's *The Nutcracker and the Mouse King* was not written for children. It was a bleak novel that examined humanity and relationships in symbolic ways. It was depressing and sometimes very hard to follow. To most adults and almost all children, the story had little redeeming value. It was hardly the kind of tale that typically becomes a Christmas classic.

In the original version of Hoffman's story, Marie was a child who lived in a home devoid of love. The only thing in the entire house that gave her joy was a Christmas gift from her Grandfather Drosselmeier, a nutcracker doll. When Marie played with the doll, it brought her great happiness. But after she had gone to bed on Christmas night, the doll conjured up some very strange dreams.

In Marie's nightmare, hundreds of mice appeared in the room. These menacing little beasts were led by a terrible creature known as the Mouse King. This seven-headed demon demanded that the girl give him her marzipan dolls. If she didn't, the Mouse King would tear her new nutcracker doll to pieces.

The child was horrified, but before she had to make a choice, the nutcracker magically came to life to battle the Mouse King. But the nutcracker was easily defeated by the Mouse King. Left with no other choice, Marie prepared to fight the despicable villain as well.

Hoffman did not describe the fight, but as the reader next witnessed Marie lying in a pool of blood, the outcome seemed obvious. Yet the little girl was horrified, as were readers, to learn that she hadn't received her injuries in the valiant battle against the Mouse King but had been severely cut while breaking into the home's doll cabinet. Her family demanded that she admit her sins and sent her to her room.

Alone and disheartened, an injured and weak Marie sulked until her grandfather came to her and told her the "real" story of the Mouse King and the nutcracker. Hoffman's next literary turn has confused almost everyone who has ever read the story.

Grandfather explained that there had been a long-standing feud between the Mouse King and the doll. It involved a beautiful princess who was cursed by the Mouse King and became incredibly ugly. The only way to reverse the curse was for a handsome man to crack the world's hardest nut with his teeth and give it to the doomed princess.

Grandfather Drosselmeier then explained that his own nephew brought the prized nut to the princess. When she ate it, she became beautiful again, but the young man grew hideously ugly. In fact, he resembled a nutcracker more than a human being.

The princess was repelled by her hero's appearance. The king banished the boy from the kingdom. As the boy left, he accidentally stepped on the Mouse King's mother, thus creating a long-lasting feud between the nutcracker and the Mouse King.

Hoffman, satisfied that he had brought the two different tales together, picked up the story where Marie's dream had ended. In this final part of the original novel, the nutcracker doll finally killed the Mouse King. The victor then swept the princess off her feet, kissed her, and took her to another land, where he became a prince. Marie then somehow met her grandfather's ugly nephew and married him. Thus, the story's central character seemed doomed to escape one loveless home for a home that offered little but ugliness and despair.

Hoffman probably wrote *The Nutcracker and the Mouse King* to present his own dark ideas about life. He seems to have believed that a majority of those who live on earth will never realize a dream and will never escape the ugliness of their day-to-day existence. It is easy to see that in its original form, this story was a fairy tale that would hardly appeal to anyone except the most cynical of readers. Thus, it's hard to imagine Hoffman's story surviving a single printing, much less becoming a Christmas classic. And it probably would have been forgotten if the tale had not received some much needed outside help.

The book's publisher decided that the original story was simply too dark and brought in famed French author Alexander Dumas to "clean it up." Dumas eliminated a great deal of the hopelessness and depression, as well as the dismal ending, and turned the basic story into a children's fairy tale. In this form, the book sold pretty well and took another step toward its status as a Christmas tradition.

In the final decade of the nineteenth century, the Dumas version of *The Nutcracker and the Mouse King* was given to the senior ballet master of the Russian Imperial Ballet. When the ballet master, Marius Petipa, read this children's story, he was convinced that it could be adapted to the stage. In 1891 he assigned one of his close friends and best writers, Pyotr Ilich Tchaikovsky, to compose the score.

Tchaikovsky was a middle-aged man who had lived a life almost as colorful as his music. The already legendary Russian composer, the son of a Russian mine inspector and a French mother, had been born on May 7, 1840. Tchaikovsky began composing in his early teens and wrote his first overture in 1862 while a student at St. Petersburg Conservatory. A decade later he won a loyal following through a dozen different productions, the most famous of which was *Swan Lake*. Yet just when his career appeared to be placing him in a position of prominence, with the likes of Mozart and Handel, the bottom fell out of his personal life. Trapped in an unhappy marriage, Tchaikovsky left his much younger wife and tried to commit suicide. Though he survived the attempt, many thought he would never come out of his depression, much less ever write again.

It took several years, but Tchaikovsky finally pulled himself out of his dark pit and regained his status as a great composer by creating the 1812 Overture, Symphony no. 5 in E Minor, and *The Sleeping Beauty*. In 1890 he even took his successful opera, *The Queen of Spades*, on a triumphant tour of the United States. Yet the Russian legend came home to find an assignment that did not intrigue or inspire him at all.

Tchaikovsky was not impressed with *The Nutcracker and the Mouse King*. He didn't like the fact that it was set at a children's Christmas party. He wanted to change the setting and revamp much of the story. Petipa stood firm in his desire to stay true to Dumas's rewrite of the original story. He even gave the protesting Tchaikovsky an exact scenario of how he thought the presentation should be written and ordered the composer to follow it. Though hardly inspired, Tchaikovsky tried to throw himself into his work. When he finally finished the music, Lev Ivanov, Petipa's assistant, choreographed the production. History tells us that Petipa and Ivanov were excited by *The Nutcracker*'s potential, while Tchaikovsky was less optimistic.

The Nutcracker ballet made its debut on December 17, 1892, at the Mariinsky Theatre in Kirov, Russia. The original cast was almost entirely made up of ballet students. Those who came to watch on opening night were hardly impressed. A reviewer, writing for the local paper, summed up the production with these words: "For dancers there is rather little in it, for art absolutely nothing, and for the artistic fate of our ballet, one more step downward."

With such bad critical reviews, *The Nutcracker* should have died quickly. But for reasons that even its famed composer did not understand, the common people loved the ballet. They came back to see it night after night. For the next forty years *The Nutcracker* was as much a part of Russian Christmas as snow and presents. Even after the communists took over the government, this element of the holidays was embraced and funded.

Almost completely unknown outside the USSR, *The Nutcracker* was finally introduced in England in 1934. It was greeted with mild enthusiasm. Six years later, with a world war raging in Europe, the Ballet Russe de Monte Carlo presented a shortened version of the ballet in the United States. The ballet still didn't create many sparks.

It was another fourteen years before the full version finally was brought to the American stage, in the midst of the Cold War. Ninety-year-old William Christensen was the force behind *The Nutcracker*'s 1954 American debut. Working with ballet master George Balanchine, Christensen took the original Russian concept and rewrote it to appeal to children. Through Christensen's American eyes, *The Nutcracker* was transformed from a staid ballet into a children's classic. It was this elderly gentleman, looking at the world with childlike vision, who created the timeless images of Mother Buffoon and her seemingly endless line of children, a Christmas tree that grows in dreams, and the Sugar Plum Fairy. *The Nutcracker* was now so different, so captivating and filled with fantasy, that when audiences saw it for the first time, they immediately fell in love with it. Even people who didn't care for ballet waited in line for hours to get tickets to this Christmas masterpiece of joy and wonder.

The American version of *The Nutcracker* quickly swept across the country and then around the world. Within a decade, it had established itself as a Christmas classic. Yet it became something more than that. *The Nutcracker* opened up the world of ballet and classical music to a new generation of children. Christmas performances of this musical masterpiece funded ballet troops in hundreds of cities around the world. Just as Dumas had breathed new life into Hoffman's original depressing story and Tchaikovsky had taken Dumas's version to a different level, Christensen's vision transformed the ballet into one almost everyone could enjoy, including the critics.

Each year more than two hundred American ballet companies pack theaters from coast to coast with their versions of *The Nutcracker*. The ballet creates the same kind of results in Europe and Asia. Hundreds of other amateur versions, just as important to *The Nutcracker*'s continuing popularity, are performed by children in towns and cities from coast to coast and border to border. Unlike Marie, whose nightmares helped create this tale, countless girls now have sweet dreams about becoming the Sugar Plum Fairy.

The Nutcracker does not embrace the scriptural story of the first Christmas. It is simply classic fantasy told in a childlike fashion. But in important ways, *The Nutcracker* accomplishes what the holidays are supposed to accomplish: it brings family and friends together to share in the wonder, joy, and magic of the season. Just like the bright-eyed expressions of twelfth-century children as their fathers cracked nuts at Christmas, the looks of wonder in children's eyes as they watch or participate in a much different holiday *Nutcracker* prove that the spirit of Christmas can be reborn in a wide variety of ways around the world each year. And that spirit is something worth celebrating.

~ 21 ~

POINSETTIAS

While the holiday season may arguably be celebrated with more fervor in North America than anywhere else on earth, the majority of the most dearly held Christmas traditions began in Europe. Americans have for the most part adopted the customs of others, rarely creating their own Christmas traditions. Yet the poinsettia, a plant that had a long and colorful history even before becoming associated with Christ's birthday, is one of the few holiday institutions that has its roots firmly planted in North American soil.

The ancient Aztecs were probably the first to note the beauty of the poinsettia. They called the plant *cuetlaxochitle*, and to this advanced civilization it represented purity. Literally, *cuetlaxochitle* means "flower that withers, mortal flower that perishes like all that is pure." The Aztecs so admired this wonderful, towering, eight-foot plant that they all but worshiped it for its beauty and majesty. Religious leaders often handled the plant and used it for medicines and dyes, but the *cuetlaxochitle* was considered so sacred that the common people were not allowed to touch it. In the Aztec culture, this plant was set apart from and above all other plants.

These legendary native Mexicans believed that the bright red color found on some of the plant's leaves was meant to serve as a reminder of the blood of the men, women, and children who had been sacrificed to appease the gods. When the plants thrived, it meant that the gods were pleased with the sacrifices the Aztecs had brought to them. During the human-sacrifice rituals, *cuetlaxochitle* plants were even brought up the mountainsides to the temple and were a vital facet of the pagan ceremony.

Botanical gardens abounded throughout the Aztec Empire. Flowers and a wide variety of herbs used by the physicians of the time were cultivated by the thousands. Of all these plants, the *cuetlaxochitle* probably meant the most to those who worked in the fields and to the ruling class who oversaw the work. Historical texts note that the gardens where the *cuetlaxochitle* grew were famed for their rich colors during the months of October to May. The Aztec leaders often strolled through these gardens, telling their sons and daughters why the *cuetlaxochitle* was so important to their culture and their gods. They pointed out that each red leaf represented a person who had given his or her life for their brothers and sisters and that as long as the Aztec people continued to remember their gods, they would, like the plant itself, flourish even during the hard winters.

In the early days of Spanish exploration, Aztec rule was

violently ended, and the civilization that the native Americans had founded was destroyed. European conquistadors, such as Cortez, had little interest in the dynamic culture they found in Mexico; they were interested only in the riches the land and its people had to offer. Thus, while the region's gold and other precious metals were shipped back to Spain, the toppled Aztec people, many of whom had been forced into slavery, fell into poverty. About the only good thing that came from this European domination was the missionary work that followed the soldiers. Compassionate Catholic priests ministered to the native people who had been trampled by those looking for wealth. The priests' Christian work was one of the few bright spots of this period.

With Spanish rule and the hard times it brought, the significance of the *cuetlaxochitle* to Mexican history was all but forgotten. In a world where just finding enough food to sustain a family for a day was the primary concern, a plant that served only as decoration was deemed unimportant. Then, in the sixteenth century, a new legend was born, and the plant once so closely identified with the human sacrifices of the Aztecs became an important facet of Christmas celebrations in Mexico.

Franciscan friars evangelizing the area of Taxco set in motion the return of the *cuetlaxochitle* to Mexican culture. The Catholic missionaries decided to teach the local people the history of the first Christmas by constructing a nativity scene. After carefully arranging the manger site, they held mass and concluded the ceremony with the breaking of a traditional piñata by the children. That was all that had been planned, but legend has it that something else happened that night that would change Mexican Christmases forever.

At some point a very poor Mexican girl named Pepita walked forward to visit the altar and view the babe in the manger. Pepita cried as she took in the scene. When concerned adults asked her what was wrong, she explained that she had no gift worthy of Jesus. She felt that if this was his birthday, he should be presented with a gift. Someone knelt beside the small girl, explaining that even the most humble gift, if given in love, would be all Christ would ask.

Pepita left the mission grounds and walked out into the country to look for a gift. She found some beautiful green weeds growing along the side of a road. After she had carefully picked them, Pepita brought them back to the nativity scene. Kneeling down in front of the crib, she offered the bouquet to baby Jesus.

Suddenly the green plant she had placed beside the manger dramatically changed. As if by divine order, the leaves turned a vivid red. Those attending the services that night believed they had witnessed a miracle. Many fell to their knees alongside the child. As the congregation prayed, one of the friars came forward and bent over to study the plant. Turning to his flock, he explained that Pepita had discovered the *flor de nochebuena*, or "flower of the blessed night." Thus, the *flor de nochebuena*, or *cuetlaxochitle*, became a Mexican symbol of Christmas and of the conversion of the area's many new Christians. From that night forward, the flower's bloom in

October signaled the coming of the Christmas season. It was a moment children and adults looked forward to as much as today's kids look forward to the first appearance of Santa Claus.

The legend of the plant was soon carried across Mexico and into other Central and South American countries. In Chiapas it was known as *sijoyo*, in Durango as *catalina*. In Guerrero, Michoscan, Veracruz, and Hidalgo it was known as *flor de Pascua*, and in Oaxaca it was called the *flor de Santa Catarina*. The people of Chile and Peru called it the "crown of the Andes," and in Argentina it is called the "federal star" and is the national flower. Yet strangely, the beautiful plant so closely associated with Christmas throughout Latin America did not migrate north. Part of the reason for this is probably that until the 1830s, Christmas was not celebrated with reverence and worship in the United States. Most churches were closed, and almost all businesses and government offices stayed open. But the influences of immigrants from Holland and Germany, as well as the impact of Dickens's *A Christmas Carol* and Moore's "The Night before Christmas," was slowly changing American culture, and Christmas as we now know it was beginning to emerge. This would eventually include the red-and-green plant as a Christmas icon. All that was needed was for someone from the United States to "discover" it.

Joel Poinsett was a multitalented man. He had studied medicine in England but had interests far beyond family practice. An amateur architect, he built a state road, a bridge with a Gothic arch, and a church in South Carolina. He was also a botanist and worked in his own greenhouses to develop new strains of existing plants and flowers. Not content to stay at home, Poinsett made a successful run for state office and became one of the young nation's most influential congressmen. President Martin Van Buren was so impressed with Poinsett that he was appointed Secretary of War, a job he held from 1836 to 1840. In this position, Poinsett invented new rockets, lobbied for a national powder factory, and fought to establish a military draft system. He also increased the size of the army by a third and oversaw the transportation of eastern Indians to the western lands. Yet in spite of all these accomplishments, it was an earlier appointment as ambassador to Mexico that would make Poinsett an American and Christmas icon.

Poinsett was not an easygoing man. He believed that he could fix anything and any situation. As an ambassador, he felt it was his duty to influence the culture rather than simply observe it. He was constantly stirring up trouble as he tried to make Mexico and Mexicans more like the United States and Americans. He offered his opinions freely and meddled in the affairs of everyone from his house servants to Latin American leaders. He caused so much dissension in Mexico that a word was even coined to describe the ambassador's intrusive conduct. That term, created from his name, was not a title of endearment. *Poinsettismo* was a word invented to describe anyone who would not keep his or her nose out of other people's business. There is little doubt that Poinsett's time in

Mexico would have been one of the worst diplomatic chapters in America's history if he had not attended a Christmas Eve service at a small Catholic church in 1824.

Poinsett was deeply affected by what he witnessed on December 24th in Santa Prisca, where the Franciscans had adorned the nativity scene with exotic red flowers. The opinionated American thought the plants gave the evening's proceedings a very elegant touch. He had never seen such a plant, and after the service, he inquired about its origin. The priests shared the legend of the Christmas plant and gave the ambassador some seeds. Poinsett shipped the seeds back to a friend in his hometown of Charleston, South Carolina. A year later, when he had so angered Mexican leaders that a price was put on his head, Poinsett went back to America. Ironically, he arrived in Washington and reported to the president on December 25th. He was immediately notified that he would no longer be needed by the State Department and was sent home.

Poinsett spent the next year working with the seeds he had obtained in Mexico. Growing new plants in his own greenhouse, he presented them to local churches in Charleston as Christmas gifts. William Prescott, a historian, horticulturist, and friend of Poinsett, wrote of the strange and exotic plants, calling them poinsettias. The name stuck, and so did the holiday use of the plant.

Among the recipients of Poinsett's initial crop was John Bartram of Philadelphia, who in turn gave the beautiful plant to Pennsylvania nurseryman Robert Buist. Buist was probably the first person to sell the plant under its Latin botanical name, *Euphorbia pulcherrima* (literally, "the most beautiful euphorbia"). Soon others were growing the Mexican plants and selling them. By the time of the Civil War, the plant, known by its new name, poinsettia, had become closely associated with an American Christmas. During the last years of his life, Poinsett succeeded in making a small fortune as a result of introducing the poinsettia to the United States, and eventually to the rest of the world.

Today it is hard to imagine Christmas without poinsettias. This plant has become a staple for decorating homes, churches, and public buildings. With its vibrant red and green leaves, this native American plant has come to be associated with Christmas for millions of people around the world. For some, the fact that the poinsettia was once revered as part of a pagan ritual of human sacrifice is troubling. Yet the meaning of the original name, *cuetlaxochitle*, "flower that withers, mortal flower that perishes like all that is pure," seems fitting for a plant representing the redeeming work of God's only begotten Son. And as a Christian symbol, with the red representing the blood that was shed on the cross and the green standing for the promise of eternal life offered to us through that sacrifice, the poinsettia can be embraced each Christmas as representing the real reason for the season.

～ 22 ～

SANTA CLAUS

Many Christians have a problem with including Santa Claus in their Christmas celebrations. Some see the jolly old elf as a competitor to Jesus. Yet Santa, unlike traditions such as Christmas trees, holly, and mistletoe, is at least partially based on Christian principles and the example of Christian men. Santa's unselfish giving, loving nature, and devotion to duty are qualities that can and should be adopted by everyone who believes that Jesus is not just the reason for the season but the path to salvation. There is nothing theological about Santa, but there is a great deal that makes him the perfect secular companion for the holy day when we stop and recognize Christ's birth.

Santa Claus's roots can be traced back to St. Nicholas of Bari. The son of wealthy parents, Nicholas was born in the fourth century in the town of Patara, Lycia (now part of Turkey). Legend records that when his parents died, the young man took all the family's money and distributed it to the needy in his hometown. He then accepted the call to full-time Christian service, becoming a monk when he was only seventeen and, shortly thereafter, a priest. The few historical records from the time indicate that he was chosen to fill the position of archbishop of Myra while he was still in his early twenties. Nicholas must have been a remarkable man, wise beyond his years and exhibiting a maturity that few gain until they are well past forty.

In the role of archbishop, Nicholas seemed to take on almost mythical heroic qualities. He was said to have saved many lives and to have been a powerful prayer warrior. Legend has it that he even had the ability to heal the sick. Yet far more than his incredible spiritual powers, it was his generosity that most endeared Nicholas to those who knew him and that made him into a legend that lives on today.

Because of his great wisdom and sensitivity, many groups throughout history have claimed Nicholas as their patron saint. Children, orphans, sailors, and even thieves looked to this compassionate saint for guidance and protection. Entire countries, including Russia and Greece, also adopted him. Thus, he is seemingly a saint for all people and all ages.

The date of Nicholas's death, December 6th, probably in the late 340s or early 350s, was one of great sadness for the people of ancient Asia Minor. But he was not forgotten. On every anniversary of his passing, his life was commemorated with an annual feast. On St. Nicholas's Eve, youngsters would set out food for Nicholas and straw for his donkey. The next morning obedient children awoke to find their gifts replaced with sweets and toys. St. Nicholas's Day is still observed in many countries, and on this day gifts are exchanged in honor of the spirit of faith, hope, and charity that he embodied.

While many trace Santa's origins back to Nicholas, another Eastern European at least partially inspired the legend of the famed Christmas elf: the Duke of Borivoy. Born in Bohemia in 907, the Duke had probably heard of Nicholas. He was a devout Catholic who spent a part of each day in church with his head bowed in prayer. At the age of fifteen, when he became one of the leaders of Bohemia after his father's death, the young man put into practice the spirit of Christian charity in every facet of his rule. He felt his calling was to reflect God in all that he did. Rather than reflecting the general spirit of the Dark Ages, the young ruler's nation was built on trust, faith, and mercy. Wanting to inspire those he ruled, the Duke of Borivoy sought out the poor and meek and shared the bounty of his kingdom with them. It became a tradition that on each Christmas Eve, he and his pages left the warm castle and tramped through deep snow to distribute food and clothing to the poor.

In spite of his kindness, the young leader was murdered by his twin brother at a church service in 929. His brother wanted to inherit the throne, and the only way this could happen was if he moved the young ruler out of the way. The duke's final words reflected his short life's work, "May God forgive you." Though he died at just twenty-two years old, the duke's spirit lived on. Stories and songs were written about the Duke of Borivoy. One of these songs, "Good King Wenceslas," is still sung today. So there can be little doubt that Wenceslas, like Nicholas, was part of the inspiration for Santa Claus.

The legend of Wenceslas was carried in a song, but St. Nicholas's story might have faded into oblivion had it not been for the tenth-century Christian author Metaphrastes. The historian collected scores of stories about Nicholas. These tales, most of them as much legend as fact, inspired a host of people to follow in the priest's generous ways. Because of Metaphrastes' stories, Christmas all across Europe would never be the same. A character resembling St. Nicholas was soon invented in each of the continent's countries.

In Germany, St. Nicholas became Weinachtsmann (Christmas man). Unlike the modern Santa, Weinachtsmann was not the principal hero of Christmas Day. He worked as a helper to the Christ child, and together they distributed gifts to children. In France, Père Noël took over Nicholas's job. He arrived each Christmas to bring special cakes, cookies, or candy. He always placed these gifts in children's shoes. In Russia, St. Nicholas evolved into Father Frost. He distributed toys in January, when the Russian church observed Christmas Day. In England, he was Father Christmas, a tall, thin, elderly man who had a long beard and carried a large sack filled with toys.

In the areas where St. Nicholas kept his identity as the bearer of gifts, a host of other characters developed as his assistants. Two of his most well-known helpers were Knecht Ruprecht and the Belsnickle. Yet strangely, both were fearsome characters, brandishing rods and switches. It was their duty not only to reward good children but also to reprove children who were naughty and couldn't recite their prayers from memory.

In some places, the images of Knecht Ruprecht and St. Nicholas merged to form Ru Klaus (Rough Nicholas, referring to his rugged appearance), Aschen Klaus (Ash Nicholas, because he carried a sack of ashes as well as a bundle of switches), and Pelznickle (Furry Nicholas, referring to his fur-clad appearance). In these cases, St. Nicholas was someone to be both loved and feared. In a very real sense, this represented the relationship most children had with their parents during this era.

Not all of St. Nicholas's companions were frightening. In fact, the Christkind (the Christ child) was thought to accompany him in many countries. Often portrayed as a fair-haired young girl, this angelic figure was sometimes the gift bearer too. She had such a gentle nature that she served to assure children that God was always with them. Yet even though the gift-giving St. Nicholas and his cousins had many fans, they also had their detractors, most of whom were members of the clergy.

After the Protestant Reformation in the sixteenth century, the veneration of Catholic saints was banned in Germany and England. But people had become accustomed to the annual visit from the gift-giving saint and didn't want to forget the purpose of the holiday. So in some countries the orders of the church were defied, and the festivities of St. Nicholas's Day were merged with Christmas celebrations. Although the gift bearer took on new, nonreligious forms, the new forms always reflected the saint's generous spirit. Still, many in England wanted to ban Nicholas and everything else that mirrored Christmas because of their pagan roots.

The unwholesome qualities of early Christmases in England made it very hard for St. Nick to gain a footing in the New World. From the time they landed on American soil in 1620, the Puritans made it illegal to mention St. Nicholas's name. People were also not allowed to sing carols, exchange gifts, or light candles at Christmastime.

More than 150 years passed before any mention of St. Nick first appeared in some American newspapers during the Christmas season, which no doubt came about due to German or Dutch influences in the New World. Though he did not make much of an impact with children or adults, a few press reports in colonial newspapers in 1773 called him St. A Claus and spoke of his impact in the homes of some immigrants.

Thirty years later, the roots of an American Christmas were established when the New York Historical Society, hearkening back to New York City's Dutch roots, recognized St. Nicholas as its patron saint. Its members also began to engage in the Dutch practice of giving gifts at Christmas. The fact that some kids were getting gifts for Christmas interested children throughout the newly formed union. Because English-speaking children found the Dutch name for St. Nicholas, Sinterklaas, strange, they uttered it so quickly that it came out Santy Claus, and thus this name became Americanized. After several more years of mispronunciation, the name evolved into Santa Claus.

In 1808 Washington Irving (the author of *Tales from Sleepy*

Hollow) wrote about Sinterklaas in his book *A History of New York*. Irving described the December visitor as a rotund little man in typical Dutch costume, with knee breeches and a broad-brimmed hat, who traveled on a flying horse-drawn wagon "dropping gifts down the chimneys of his favorites" on the Eve of St. Nicholas. The familiar phrase "laying his finger beside his nose" first appeared in Irving's story.

While Irving opened the door for children's gifts to be delivered in December, it was a professor of theology who ultimately made Christmas a holiday whose light shined directly on the faces of children in the United States. In writing "A Visit from St. Nicholas" (now known as "The Night Before Christmas"), Clement Clarke Moore would also establish the tradition of Santa Claus arriving not on St. Nicholas Eve or on January 6th, the day of Epiphany, but on December 24th, Christmas Eve.

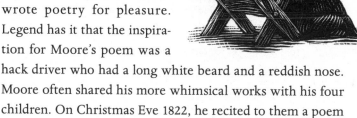

Moore, who was a bishop of the Episcopal Church in New York City and a professor at General Theological Seminary, wrote poetry for pleasure. Legend has it that the inspiration for Moore's poem was a hack driver who had a long white beard and a reddish nose. Moore often shared his more whimsical works with his four children. On Christmas Eve 1822, he recited to them a poem that would change the face of American Christmas forever.

Supposedly Moore didn't want his name attached to the poem; he believed it would hurt his status as a university educator. But a family member or a friend took the poem to the local paper the next year and had it published. Moore's poem described Santa as a jolly old elf who flew around in a miniature sleigh with eight tiny reindeer. Moore even identified the reindeer by the names we still know today and invented the method by which Santa returns up the chimney. Yet it was the fact that this St. Nick visited girls and boys on Christmas Eve that would change Christmas forever.

The Night Before Christmas
By Clement Clarke Moore

'Twas the night before Christmas, when all through the house
Not a creature was stirring, not even a mouse;
The stockings were hung by the chimney with care,
In hopes that St. Nicholas soon would be there;
The children were nestled all snug in their beds,
While visions of sugar-plums danced in their heads;
And Mamma in her 'kerchief, and I in my cap,
Had just settled our brains for a long winter's nap;
When out on the lawn there arose such a clatter,
I sprang from the bed to see what was the matter.
Away to the window I flew like a flash,
Tore open the shutters and threw up the sash.
The moon on the breast of the new-fallen snow,
Gave the lustre of mid-day to objects below,

Santa Claus

When, what to my wondering eyes should appear,
But a miniature sleigh, and eight tiny rein-deer,
With a little old driver, so lively and quick,
I knew in a moment it must be St. Nick.
More rapid than eagles his coursers they came,
And he whistled, and shouted, and called them by name;
"Now, Dasher! now, Dancer! now, Prancer and Vixen!
On, Comet! on, Cupid! on, Donder and Blitzen!
To the top of the porch! to the top of the wall!
Now dash away! dash away! dash away all!"
As dry leaves that before the wild hurricane fly,
When they meet with an obstacle, mount to the sky;
So up to the house-top the coursers they flew,
With the sleigh full of toys, and St. Nicholas too.
And then, in a twinkling, I heard on the roof,
The prancing and pawing of each little hoof—
As I drew in my head, and was turning around,
Down the chimney St. Nicholas came with a bound.
He was dressed all in fur, from his head to his foot,
And his clothes were all tarnished with ashes and soot;
A bundle of toys he had flung on his back,
And he look'd like a peddler just opening his pack.
His eyes—how they twinkled! his dimples how merry!
His cheeks were like roses, his nose like a cherry!
His droll little mouth was drawn up like a bow,
And the beard of his chin was as white as the snow;
The stump of a pipe he held tight in his teeth,

And the smoke it encircled his head like a wreath;
He had a broad face and a little round belly,
That shook when he laughed, like a bowl full of jelly.
He was chubby and plump, a right jolly old elf,
And I laughed when I saw him, in spite of myself;
A wink of his eye and a twist of his head,
Soon gave me to know I had nothing to dread;
He spoke not a word, but went straight to his work,
And fill'd all the stockings; then turned with a jerk,
And laying his finger aside of his nose,
And giving a nod, up the chimney he rose;
He sprang to his sleigh, to his team gave a whistle,
And away they all flew like the down of a thistle.
But I heard him exclaim, ere he drove out of sight,
"Happy Christmas to all, and to all a good night."

Moore's poem instantly made Santa an American Christmas institution. Yet what did the jolly old elf look like? Moore hadn't really described Santa. For all anyone knew, he could be short, tall, fat, skinny, old, or young. He could be any color, have a beard or be clean-shaven, and wear anything from buckskins to a lawyer's suit. Thus, in the 1840s, when department stores began to hire individuals to appear as Santa, the gift giver appeared in a wide variety of costumes. It seemed that Santa had more looks than he had reindeer.

In 1863 Thomas Nast, a German immigrant, began to define the look of the "real" Mr. Claus. Nast was the famed illustrator and caricaturist who created the donkey and elephant images that depicted the Democratic and Republican political parties. He was also on the staff of *Harper's Weekly* from 1860 until the late 1880s. When Nast was asked to illustrate Moore's "The Night Before Christmas" for a book of children's poems, he gave the world a Santa who was far less stern looking than the ecclesiastical St. Nicholas of Europe. And while Santa was drawn as an elfin figure in red, there was something very human about him. This Santa was kind, gentle, and jolly. Therefore it was all the more ironic that Nast patterned his generous Santa after the industrial "robber barons" of the American ruling class. The artist did this as a social statement, an indirect ploy to get those who had profited from the American way of life to give back to the poor who had made them wealthy. Most of the industrialists failed to catch Nast's symbolic imagery, but America's weary president certainly knew how to make the image work for the cause of the North during the Civil War.

Abraham Lincoln was so impressed with this new Santa that he asked Nast to draw the elf visiting with Federal troops around a battlefield campfire on Christmas Eve. The president wanted children on both sides of the Mason-Dixon line to know that Santa Claus stood for the preservation of the Union. It is said that Nast's drawing had a dynamic affect on morale in the North during that long, cold, and bloody winter.

For twenty-two years, Nast added more and more details to his drawings of Santa in each of *Harper's Weekly*'s December issues. He enhanced the legend of Santa Claus and fleshed out the life of the man who was filling stockings from coast to coast. Nast drew Santa's workshop, created the "naughty and nice" list, and, in 1885, sketched the home of the man in red. In that year's illustration, Nast presented two children looking at a map of the world and tracing Santa's journey from the North Pole to the United States. The following year, the American writer George P. Webster built on this bit of genius, explaining that Santa's toy factory and home were hidden in the ice and snow of the North Pole.

Yet sadly, in a nation where many families were poor, Santa didn't call on everyone. The fact that so many children had never received a Christmas gift led to classroom debates on the existence of the jolly man with the beard. In 1897 a little girl named Virginia O'Hanlon listened to some of her classmates who had never received gifts from Santa and began to have doubts about the reality of Santa. In a 1933 interview, she recalled the events that led to one of the most famous editorials of all time.

Quite naturally I believed in Santa Claus, for he had never disappointed me. But when less fortunate little boys and girls said there wasn't any Santa Claus, I was filled with doubts. I asked my father, and he was a little evasive on the subject.

It was a habit in our family that whenever any doubts came up as to how to pronounce a word or some question of historical fact was in doubt, we wrote to the "Question and Answer" column in *The New York Sun*. Father would always say, "If you see it in *The Sun*, it's so," and that settled the matter.

"Well, I'm just going to write The Sun and find out the real truth," I said to father.

He said, "Go ahead, Virginia. I'm sure The Sun will give you the right answer, as it always does."

The third grader wrote the *Sun*, put the letter into an envelope, and mailed it to the editorial department. What happened next would make newspaper history.

Dear Editor—

I am 8 years old. Some of my little friends say there is no Santa Claus.

Papa says, "If you see it in *The Sun*, it's so." Please tell me the truth, is there a Santa Claus?

Virginia O'Hanlon

Virginia's letter passed through several hands before it found its way to veteran editor Francis P. Church. The son of a Baptist minister, Church had covered the Civil War for the *New York Times* and had been on the staff of the *New York Sun* for twenty years. Like the other staff members who had been handed Virginia's letter, the editor wondered how he could answer the letter. After all, the *Sun* was a newspaper that proudly declared it printed nothing but the truth. As he read and reread Virginia's letter, he knew this would be his toughest assignment in his long newspaper career.

A few days later, Virginia was thrilled to find her letter and the reply on the editorial page of the daily newspaper. Church had no idea that what he wrote would become the most remembered and beloved editorial ever penned.

Virginia, your little friends are wrong. They have been affected by the skepticism of a skeptical age. They do not believe except they see. They think that nothing can be which is not comprehensible by their little minds. All minds, Virginia, whether they be men's or children's, are little. In this great universe of ours, man is a mere insect, an ant, in his intellect as compared with the boundless world about him, as measured by the intelligence capable of grasping the whole of truth and knowledge.

Yes, Virginia, there is a Santa Claus. He exists as certainly as love and generosity and devotion exist, and you know that they abound and give to your life its highest beauty and joy. Alas! how dreary would be the world if there were no Santa Claus! It would be as dreary as if there were no Virginias. There would be no childlike faith then, no poetry, no romance to make tolerable this existence. We should have no enjoyment, except in sense and sight. The external light with which childhood fills the world would be extinguished.

Not believe in Santa Claus! You might as well not believe in fairies. You might get your papa to hire men to watch in all the chimneys on Christmas eve to catch Santa Claus, but even if you did not see Santa Claus coming down, what would that prove? Nobody sees Santa Claus, but that is no sign that there is no Santa Claus. The most real things in the world are those that neither children nor men can see. Did you ever see fairies dancing on the lawn? Of course not, but that's no proof that they are not there. Nobody can conceive or imagine all the wonders there are unseen and unseeable in the world.

You tear apart the baby's rattle and see what makes the noise inside, but there is a veil covering the unseen world which not the strongest man, nor even the united strength of all the strongest men that ever lived could tear apart. Only faith, poetry, love, romance, can push aside that curtain and view and picture the supernal beauty and glory beyond. Is it all real? Ah, Virginia, in all this world there is nothing else real and abiding.

No Santa Claus! Thank God! he lives and lives forever. A thousand years from now, Virginia, nay 10 times 10,000 years from now, he will continue to make glad the heart of childhood.

Virginia O'Hanlon went on to graduate from Hunter College and to earn a master's degree from Columbia. She taught in the New York City school system for forty-seven years. When she retired, the *Sun* was still running her letter every Christmas on its front page.

Santa received his final makeover from artist Haddon Sundblom. Beginning in 1931, Sundblom's billboards, magazine ads, and in-store displays for Coca-Cola featured a portly, grandfatherly Santa with human proportions and a ruddy complexion. Sundblom's cheery Santa replaced Nast's image, which was a bit harsher and not as smoothly drawn, as the Santa for the ages. Today almost every drawing and living representation of the jolly old elf looks like the man Sundbolm drew for the soft-drink giant. There can be little doubt that this Santa is one of the most recognizable images in the entire world.

In the years since the first publication of Moore's "The Night Before Christmas," Santa got another reindeer, Rudolph, who has appeared in countless other books, movies, and television programs, and who has grown into an icon that means as much to the image of Christmas as the tree, stockings, and gifts. Yet what so many have forgotten is that while the appearance of Santa Claus was invented by men, Santa's heart and spirit were inspired by the love and generosity of Christians such as St. Nicholas and Wenceslas. Each gift that the man in the red suit gives is a living testament to the men who gave because they felt called by God to reach out to the needy around them. In a very real sense, Santa is the living embodiment of the wonderful children's hymn "Jesus Loves the Little Children." Like Jesus, Santa loves them all!

~ 23 ~

STOCKINGS

The legend of hanging Christmas stockings may be most familiar in the words of a line from Clement Clarke Moore's classic Christmas poem: "The stockings were hung by the chimney with care, in hopes that St. Nicholas soon would be there." But hanging stockings is actually one of the oldest Christmas traditions—even though this tradition originated not as a part of the celebration of Christ's birth but rather as a tribute to a priest.

Christmas stockings today are often quite large, usually have names written on them, and are rarely a piece of clothing that can be worn in public. The modern Christmas stocking is often just another ornament, something to hang from the mantel or wall simply because it has always been done that way. In the twenty-first century, the grand presents that most children wish for at Christmas could scarcely be held in a simple sock, and most kids would be dismayed if all they could claim on Christmas morning fit into the old stocking hung by the fireplace. Yet in ancient times, particularly in Eastern

Europe, the stocking hanging by the fire was an essential part of each child's December dreams.

The legend of the stocking was born out of a mundane but necessary nightly ritual. During the Great Depression, but dating back thousands of years before America existed, many families were forced to wash out their clothes each night and hang them by the fire to dry so that they could wear the items the next day. Only the wealthy had a closet filled with clothes. This was especially true of socks and stockings. Poor children rarely had more than one pair. These stockings were therefore taken care of as if they were one of the most precious items on earth. And in the cold winters of Eastern Europe, a warm pair of socks was essential. Hence, stockings hung on the mantel each night were not a Christmas tradition, but rather a daily ritual in both America and Europe.

During the fourth century, a priest named Nicholas ministered to the poor families throughout his hometown of Patara and the area around Bari (in what is now Turkey). The son of rich parents, this remarkable man, who would become an archbishop while still in his twenties, felt a particular calling to reach out to the poor. Be it through gifts or kind words, he was constantly finding ways to make the lives of children better.

The tenth-century Christian author Metaphrastes records that while on a trip to attend a meeting outside his parish, Nicholas heard about a widower and his three teenage daughters who lived in the town where Nicholas was staying. The impoverished man and his family were literally starving to death. Things had gotten so bad that the father was even considering selling a daughter into slavery. He reasoned that if he sold one child, he might be able to raise enough money to have dowries for the other two. With the dowries, the girls could be married and escape the poverty and hunger that was characteristic of their daily lives. Without dowries, they would never marry and would be doomed to continue their life in abject poverty.

Even though the widower made the arrangements to sell his oldest daughter, when it came time to close the deal, the father could not part with even one of his daughters. He viewed his inability to complete the transaction as dooming all three girls to a hopeless life of despair. Hungry, tired, and depressed, the man prayed for help. He had no way of knowing that as he looked to God, Nicholas had already heard of his plight.

As was their custom each evening, the girls each washed their one pair of stockings and hung them by the fire to dry overnight. Then they went to bed. The father turned in soon thereafter. Sometime after midnight, someone silently opened a window and tossed a gold piece into one of the stockings. The oldest daughter discovered the coin the next day as she dressed. She took it to her father, who looked to heaven and thanked God for the miracle.

That first gold coin became the oldest daughter's dowry. After she was married, a coin astonishingly appeared in the second daughter's stockings. The remarkable event was repeated again for the youngest child as well.

Naturally the news of the magical appearance of the money in the stockings quickly became known throughout the community. Most believed it to be a gift straight from heaven, but a few noted that the priest Nicholas had been in town each time money was found. They also pointed to the generosity of the clergyman as proof that he was the real source of the gifts that kept the family together. Either way, many others wanted to become a part of this magical experience. Throughout the land, men, women, and children began to search their stockings each morning for gifts. They looked especially hard whenever Nicholas happened to be visiting their village.

When Nicholas died sometime around 350, the date of his death, December 6th, soon became known as St. Nicholas's Day. On this day, because of the story of the father and his three daughters, children hung out stockings. It was almost always the case that the next morning they found treats inside the stockings. Thus, in the earliest recorded accounts, it was St. Nicholas, not Christmas, that was associated with the hanging of stockings. Stockings would become a part of Christmas lore much later.

In 1823 Clement Clarke Moore's poem "A Visit from St. Nicholas," later to be known as "The Night Before Christmas," was published. Moore made use of the legend of St. Nicholas, complete with the hanging of stockings, but transferred the date of his visit from St. Nicholas's Eve, a holiday that was not then acknowledged in America, to "the night before Christmas." Thus, with the simple stroke of a pen, hanging stockings by the tree or on the mantel quickly became a Christmas tradition that children all over the world annually observed on December 24th.

Initially, during the first hundred years after Moore wrote the poem we now know as "The Night Before Christmas," Santa deposited almost all of the presents into stockings. Soon children sensed that the size of their foot determined the generosity of the old man from the North Pole and began to hang larger and larger socks by the fireplace. With the invention of electricity and the toy trains that followed, a child's Christmas dreams could no longer be held by a simple sock. But the stockings were still hung each year, even though Santa often no longer filled them.

Today, when the stockings are filled, it is often with candy or money instead of gifts. Some people still cling to the old tradition of placing an orange in the stocking. The orange symbolizes the gold of Nicholas's gift to the poor father and his three daughters. Others have expanded the legend to include a walnut for good luck and an apple for health. A small number of people even leave sweets in the stocking for children who have been good and rocks for those who have not. And in some cases, a chunk of coal, considered a treasured gift a century ago, marks a child who has been naughty rather than nice. Yet empty or filled, stockings remain a vital part of the Christmas season.

While the stockings hung each year are rarely ones that are worn, and while these Christmas decorations are most often bought, not homemade, what they stand for should be as treasured in a modern Christmas as it was by the poor widower and his daughters more than sixteen hundred years ago. Christmas is a time of giving, not just to friends and family, but also to those who are suffering, poor, and hopeless. Empty stockings hung at home or unsold stockings in stores should remind everyone who celebrates the birth of Christ to search for ways to make the season bright for others who have not been as blessed. St. Nicholas didn't just hear about a family in need; he responded. Without the priest's action, there would be no Christmas stockings, and the most special time of year would be missing one its most beloved elements. Nicholas provided the example, and the Christmas stocking provides a means to spread the reason for the season far and wide.

~ 24 ~

THE TWELVE DAYS
OF CHRISTMAS

To many people, the lyrics of the song "The Twelve Days of Christmas" seem strange beyond belief. The odd carol's words might make one think it is a novelty song, in the vein of "Grandma Got Run Over by a Reindeer." Though a host of modern internet sites and some magazine articles have tried to reduce "The Twelve Days of Christmas" to little more than a silly Christmas carol, in fact most scholars of the Catholic Church deem it a very important surviving example of a time when that denomination used codes to disguise their teachings. Originally a poem written by Catholic clerics, this song was transformed into a carol at a time when celebrating the twelve days of Christmas was one of the most important holiday customs. By understanding why the clerics chose the twelve days as a wrapping for their poem, the full impact of the lost tradition of the twelve days of Christmas can be understood.

Teaching the Catholic faith was outlawed in sixteenth-century England. Those who instructed their children in Catholicism could be drawn and quartered. Thus, the church went underground. To hide the important and illegal elements of their teaching, clerics composed poems that seemed silly to most people. But these verses were veiled works that taught the church's most important tenets. "The Twelve Days of Christmas" is said to be one of these teaching tools.

Before translating the code locked inside this poem that became a carol, one needs to know the dates of the twelve days of Christmas and why they were important long before Britain outlawed all religions except the one endorsed by the king. Most people today believe that the twelve days of Christmas start on December 12th or 13th and run through Christmas Eve or Christmas Day. But in fact, the first day of Christmas is December 25th and the final day is January 5th. Thus, for hundreds of years the Christmas holidays didn't begin until Christmas Eve and didn't end until Epiphany.

Why were these twelve days important? These dozen days were tied to more than just the teaching of the Catholic Church. A host of other denominations also celebrated the twelve days of Christmas. Some denominations celebrated Christmas in January and began to count the twelve days then. But whenever they began, the counting of the days became an important facet of each holiday season. Even in the Dark Ages, in some Eastern European churches the twelve days of Christmas meant attending daily church services. For Christians who lived during this extremely difficult age, the twelve days were a time of rededication and renewal. It was also a period when small, simple, and usually symbolic gifts of faith were given to children. Thus, in both coded poems and public worship, the twelve days were considered a holy period.

For many Christians today, even the recognition of the twelve days of Christmas has been lost, for two reasons. The first is that when Epiphany lost out to Christmas as the day of giving gifts, many simply quit celebrating the twelve-day observance. The other reason is based more on the change in the fabric of culture than on overlooking the Christian holiday of Epiphany.

In ancient times, when most societies were rural, few people worked in the dead of winter. It was a time when many were spending long, dark days inside their homes, looking forward to winter's chill giving way to the spring thaw. So devoting a dozen days to prayer, reflection, and attending church was not a huge undertaking. Yet with the coming of the Industrial Age and the regular year-round work schedules it brought, finding time to continue the activities that had been traditionally associated with the twelve days of Christmas became all but impossible for most people. So the passing of the twelve-days custom probably had as much to do with "progress" as with anything else. As fewer and fewer churches and families participated in the tradition, it was all but lost. Yet in the obscure poem that was later turned into a popular carol, "The Twelve Days of Christmas" live on. And the twelve days described are actually a wonderful and complete picture of the Christian faith.

The "true love" mentioned in the song is not a sweetheart but the Catholic Church's code for God. The person who receives the gifts represents anyone who has accepted Christ as the Son of God and as Savior. And each of the gifts portrays an important facet of the story of true faith.

&

On the first day of Christmas my true love gave to me. . . . a partridge in a pear tree. The partridge in a pear tree represents Jesus, the Son of God, whose birthday we celebrate on the first day of Christmas. Christ is symbolically presented as a mother partridge, the only bird that will die to protect its young.

On the second day of Christmas my true love gave to me. . . . two turtledoves. These twin birds represent the Old and New Testaments. So in this gift, the singer finds the complete story of Judeo-Christian faith and God's plan for the world. The doves are the biblical roadmap that is available to everyone.

On the third day of Christmas my true love gave to me. . . . three French hens. These birds represent faith, hope, and love. This gift hearkens back to 1 Corinthians 13, the love chapter written by the apostle Paul.

On the fourth day of Christmas my true love gave to me. . . . four calling birds. One of the easiest facets of the song's code to figure out, these fowl are the four Gospels—Matthew, Mark, Luke, and John.

On the fifth day of Christmas my true love gave to me. . . . five gold rings. The gift of the rings represents the first five books of the Old Testament, known as the Torah or the Pentateuch.

On the sixth day of Christmas my true love gave to me. . . . six geese a-laying. These lyrics can be traced back to the first story found in the Bible. Each egg is a day in creation, a time when the world was "hatched" or formed by God.

On the seventh day of Christmas my true love gave to me. . . . seven swans a-swimming. It would take someone quite familiar with the Bible to identify this gift. Hidden in the code are the seven gifts of the Holy Spirit: prophecy, ministry, teaching, exhortation, giving, leading, and compassion. As swans are one of the most beautiful and graceful creatures on earth, they would seem to be a perfect symbol for the spiritual gifts.

On the eighth day of Christmas my true love gave to me. . . . eight maids a-milking. As Christ came to save even the lowest of the low, this gift represents the ones who would receive his word and accept his grace. Being a milkmaid was about the worst job one could have in England during this period; this code conveyed that Jesus cared as much about servants as he did those of royal blood. The eight who were blessed included the poor in spirit, those who mourn, the meek, those who hunger and thirst for righteousness, the merciful, the pure in heart, the peacemakers, and those who are persecuted for righteousness' sake.

On the ninth day of Christmas my true love gave to me. . . . nine ladies dancing. These nine dancers were really the gifts known as the fruit of the Spirit. The fruits are love, joy, peace, patience, kindness, generosity, faithfulness, gentleness, and self-control.

On the tenth day of Christmas my true love gave to me. . . . ten lords a-leaping. This is probably the easiest gift to understand. As lords were judges and in charge of the law, this code for the Ten Commandments was fairly straightforward to Catholics.

On the eleventh day of Christmas my true love gave to me. . . . eleven pipers piping. This is almost a trick question, as most think of the disciples in terms of a dozen. But when Judas betrayed Jesus and committed suicide, there were only eleven men who carried out the gospel message.

On the twelfth day of Christmas my true love gave to me. . . . twelve drummers drumming. The final gift is tied directly to the Catholic Church. The drummers are the twelve points of doctrine in the Apostles' Creed. "I believe in God, the Father almighty, creator of heaven and earth. I believe in Jesus Christ, his only Son, our Lord. He was conceived by the power of the Holy Spirit and born of the Virgin Mary. He suffered under Pontius Pilate, was crucified, died, and was buried. He descended into hell. On the third day he rose again. He ascended into heaven, and is seated at the right hand of the Father. He will come again to judge the living and the dead. I believe in the Holy Spirit, the holy catholic Church, the communion of saints, the forgiveness of sins, the resurrection of the body, and life everlasting."

A silly song? On the surface, perhaps, but in reality a refreshing reminder of the essential elements of Christian faith.

The twelve days of Christmas may no longer be a recognized holiday tradition, but the days were an important bridge that connected persecuted believers of the past with the whole story of God's plan. In the complicated world of today, a trip back to the not-so-distant past when Christians celebrated the twelve days of Christmas would probably enhance the meaning of Christmas for everyone.

25

XMAS

Over the past sixty years or so, Christians have lamented the commercialization of Christmas. Many have pointed to magazines, newspapers, and store advertisements that seem to pull Jesus out of the holidays by substituting an *X* in place of the name Christ in the word Christmas. While it is usually true that those who use Xmas these days are doing so to save space and shorten the word, Xmas is hardly a new concept—or an irreverent one. Its use actually dates back to the earliest days of the Christian church.

Many of the Gentiles who became the initial followers of Christ were Greek. The Greek for Christ's name is *Xristos* (pronounced *Christos*). While it is well known that a fish was often used as a symbol to denote churches and Christian gathering places during the ancient days of the church, many Greeks also used the letter *X* (pronounced *chi*) as their symbol of faith. This *X* marked the places where they worshiped. Therefore, the use of the letter X for Christ is one of the oldest traditions of the Christian faith—one of the first concrete symbols that signified the gospel message for people of all races and backgrounds. Knowing that Greeks were following the teachings of a Jewish man was almost mind-boggling to scores of pagans during this time. It also spoke volumes about the nature of Christianity—that all were welcome to become part of the family of God.

The apostle Paul no doubt knew what the symbol *X* meant. He had led a large number of his Greek brothers and sisters to Christ. A majority of those who called the Savior *Xristos* financially supported Paul's missionary work and created an environment for the rapid growth of Christianity in Europe. Many of these Greeks were so enthused about their faith that they helped ignite a fire that rapidly spread the word to the far corners of the known world. Yet they paid a price as well.

Countless Greek Christians were persecuted for their faith. They were stoned, hanged, burned, and put to death in grotesque displays in Rome's Colosseum. When a Christian was martyred, other Christians often traced an *X* to mark the spot where a true believer had given his or her life in faithfulness to Christ. Hence, in the initial days of Christianity, *X* was also the ultimate symbol of devotion and sacrifice.

During the early days of the church, Xmas did not exist. This was not because church leaders felt that using such a term would be a sign of disrespect. Since carving letters into the stones of homes and churches was not an easy chore, having an *X* stand for the meeting place of Christians was fine with the clergy. The reason that Xmas was not employed during the holiday season was that there *was* no holiday season. It would be almost three and a half centuries before the church designated a date to celebrate Christ's birth, and even then Christmas was not a widely recognized holiday.

Many of the early Christians had a basic education and could read. But as time passed and the missionary movement spread the gospel across Europe, converts to the faith were largely unschooled. These men and women would not have recognized their own names on a document, much less the name of Jesus Christ. Therefore, symbols became an important part of faith during the Dark Ages. Some members of the clergy taught new converts that *X* was a symbol for Christ. By writing the *X*, a man, woman, or child could easily spell out in one simple symbol what defined his or her faith.

During the sixteenth century, as more and more European clergymen began to document the history of Christianity and to record the day-to-day business of the church, the use of an *X* for Christ was again widely employed. It was during this time that the word "Xmas" first began to appear in the writings of Catholic clerics and monks. Christ's name was probably abbreviated in this manner for three reasons. The first was that almost all religious documents of the time were handwritten in a very ornate style. A large *X* could be drawn in a much more artistic fashion than could the spelled-out name of Christ. Thus, by writing Xmas with dramatic flair, the day of Christ's birth stood out.

The second reason probably was that ink and paper were not as easy to come by as they are today. Hence, shortening any word would save not only time but also precious resources.

Ultimately, however, the primary reason many of the Christian writers of the time used Xmas was no doubt because of their knowledge of the Greek language and the early history of the church. In the minds of these men, Xmas was a word of power that contained great devotional value. It was a term that honored both the early Christian followers, many of whom became martyrs, and the Savior they had chosen to lead them. The clerics wanted to make sure that believers remembered the fallen heroes of the faith each Christmas.

As time went on, and reaching a more educated public with a deeper understanding of what faith meant became more important, Xmas was again used by the church. This time the term was employed to point out that while Christ's birth was necessary and was a cause for great celebration, it was his death and resurrection that gave real meaning to the Christian faith. Therefore, the *X* in Xmas reminded believers not only of Christ's birth but also of the most important Christian symbol, the cross.

When Christmas finally evolved into a holiday with commercial significance in the mid-1800s, retailers began to note the use of Xmas by certain small Christian groups. In order to save print space and make their flyers and advertisements easier to read, stores picked up on this term based on a very old symbol. It also made sense because in those days many Americans could not read. It was far easier for them to understand the meaning of the word Xmas than to grasp a longer word like Christmas.

Today, in a culture where few know Greek and almost everyone has a working knowledge of English, the need for employing the symbols of faith is not widely needed. Hence, most Christians don't know that Xmas was first used by the church and not invented as a shortcut used by merchants during the commercialization of the holiday season. The fact that the knowledge of the real meaning of X has slipped away from most Christian teachings is a great loss. The early Greek believers did not know the joy of worshiping freely. They did not celebrate Christ's birth publicly. They often paid for their faith with their lives. Yet they helped spread the gospel to the far corners of their world. To them, living under the sign of X—the sign of Christ—was the ultimate statement of faith. If they could visit today's world and see the term Xmas, they would immediately understand its correlation with the Son of God. Thus, to them, Xmas would be one of the most wonderful and powerful traditions of the modern Christmas.

~ 26 ~

YULE LOGS

The word "yule" was first used to describe an ancient Viking ritual that celebrated the winter solstice. Yule is derived from the Norse word *jul*, which means "wheel." *Jul* was probably chosen to describe the ritual because many Norse people viewed their calendar as a wheel slowly turning through the seasons. Living in regions where oppressive darkness ruled for much of the winter, these Nordic people naturally celebrated mightily when the shortest day of the year ended on December 20th. The passing of this date led to longer days, more light and warmth, and the promise of summer.

As a part of the solstice celebration, the Vikings would cut a huge log, drag it back to the village, and set it afire. This "yule log" was supposed to drive away evil spirits, bring good luck to the people of the area, and welcome the sun back to the skies. In the process of doing all these things, the fire probably took a bit of the chill out of the cold winter air too. Though the burning of the log during the winter solstice is now almost always associated with the ancient people of

Scandinavia, they probably borrowed the custom from earlier civilizations.

Cleopatra was surely familiar with the custom of log burning during what is now known as December, as Moses probably was. The Egyptians had a custom of burning logs for the celebration of the winter solstice during the lives of these two historical icons and dating back to 5000 BC. In Egypt the flames of these fires honored the sun god Horus. The Sumerians burned similar logs during the final days of winter, as did a host of smaller groups.

Thirty years after the death of Christ, Roman culture adopted Mithras, the Persian sun god. Starting in the fifth decade of the first century, the citizens of Rome burned a log during the initial ten days of the Saturnalia festival to usher in another year of the strong rule of Mithras. Throughout history, other groups living in Europe and Asia burned large logs during the solstice as well, but it was the Vikings who put and kept the yule log on the map.

When the Vikings invaded Britain during the Dark Ages, they brought their customs with them. One that caught on was the burning of the yule log. The first to pick up on this winter tradition were the Celtic Druids. The Celts had long had a feast as part of their celebration of the winter solstice. The Druids called the solstice Midwinter or Fionn's Day. As trees were important in the Celts' religious beliefs, particularly the oak, it was only natural for them to incorporate the yule log into their rituals. In some villages, where the oak represented life and the pine tree stood for death, a log from each tree was set afire at the same time. The wood that burned the longest indicated the fate of those who lived in the village.

In the fourth century the ceremonies began to move indoors, and Celts and Gaelic Europeans dragged into their homes logs large enough to fill their hearths. They anointed this timber with salt, holly, wine, and spices. Then they lit the wood with a piece of the previous year's yule log. After the fire had burned out, the ashes were kept as a protective shield from evil. Some Celts even tossed some of the ashes outside their homes to guard their houses from lightning strikes.

At about the same time that the Celts and Vikings were burning yule logs in Britain and Scandinavia, many Christians in Eastern Europe were calling the celebration of Christmas the Feast of Lights. During this festival, these believers burned a log to symbolize the end of the world's darkness and the coming of God's child to bring eternal light and life to the world. While not influenced by or associated in any way with the Viking practice of the yule celebration, the Feast of the Lights probably paved the way for another group of men in England to Christianize the custom of burning a yule log.

Because the Druids and the Vikings worshiped Thor, it would have gone against everything the Christian Teutonic knights stood for to accept the yule-log custom as one of their own. Yet as these Christian soldiers surely knew of the eastern European custom of burning a log during the Feast of Lights, this pagan yule ritual probably seemed familiar to them. So the knights not only sanctioned the custom but were the primary reason that it soon came to mean so much to Christians around the world.

In the legend, probably first created by the knights and the clergy who rode with them, the ceremonial burning of the yule log came to symbolize the Christian vision of good versus evil. As the fire grew brighter and burned hotter, and as the log turned into ashes, it symbolized Christ's final and ultimate triumph over sin. For the next six centuries, this Christian yule custom would spread and grow. By the time the Normans invaded England in 1066, the celebration had been fully incorporated into most British communities.

For the next seven hundred years, English families were expected to find their own yule log. It could not be purchased, and it had to be cut on the family's or a close friend's property. The log was to be chopped down in the late winter or early spring. It was also the custom for this large tree to be dragged home by those who were going to burn it. As the original tradition called for the log to burn for the entire twelve days of Christmas, it had to be huge. Often it took a team of oxen to accomplish the monumental task of log relocation. When it arrived at the home, it was placed outside to dry.

During the year of drying, the log was often rubbed with spices, rum, and wine, thus assuring that the smell that would emanate from the fire the next Christmas would fill the house with an appealing odor. This perfume-like odor was to remind everyone of the spice gifts of the Magi, the "sweet" life Christ had lived, and the precious gift he had given by dying on the cross to cancel humankind's debt of sins. The log had great importance in the life of each family, and as it dried out, it was attended to as regularly as were the crops and the livestock.

On Christmas Eve the family finally brought the log into the home, carrying the lumber around the kitchen three times before finally placing it in the hearth. Dried holly leaves were stuffed under the log for kindling and more spices were packed around it. When the preparation was finished, each household waited for the signal that began the celebration of the twelve days of Christmas.

When the church bells sounded on Christmas Eve, the lady of the home retrieved from underneath her bed a small stick or piece of kindling from the previous year's log. The woman had carefully packed this remnant away. She took this wood back to the fireplace and set it aside. As only those who were pure were to light the fire, she then washed her hands. Any dirt on the hand that held the starting  flame would have been seen as a sign of great disrespect, so the task of washing was never taken lightly.

Before the woman could again pick up her stick and light the fire, her husband splashed holy water, obtained from the church, onto the log. A general prayer was said. Then the husband poured three glasses of wine over the log; one for the Father, one for the Son, and one for the Holy Ghost. Another prayer was said, this one specifically asking that the fire would warm the home, that God would provide the family with enough food for the year, and that everyone in the household would someday experience the peace to be found in heaven. Only after the completion of these ceremonial rituals could the wife finally take her kindling, light it from a candle, and prepare to place it against the log. As she did, the entire family held its breath.

It was said that the new yule log had to catch fire during the first attempt at lighting. If it did not, it was a sign that great misfortune would soon befall a member of the family. One can imagine the extreme pressure the woman of the house felt as she went about her assigned duties. In her mind, the fate of her husband and children were in her hands.

Once the fire was safely started, the fun began. Everyone would pitch a sprig of holly into the flames as a symbolic act of burning up the past year's troubles and as a way of asking forgiveness for past sins. The Christmas story was told next, and everyone was reminded that the light from the fire stood for the life that God sent to earth through his Son. Games were then played, songs were sung, and stories told. Cider was given to each member of the household, and toasts were made to faith and prosperity. Finally a huge meal, prepared over the heat from the yule log, was eaten.

The next twelve days were filled not only with the wonder

of the season but also with a great deal of hard work. The women of the household, the mother and her daughters, took turns tending the log. It was considered bad luck for the fire to go out before the end of the twelve days of Christmas. If the yule log went out or burned up too soon, the household was doomed to bad luck for the next year. It was also necessary for the women to save a small piece of the yule log for use during the following Christmas.

As the centuries passed, the English custom was exported around the world, including to America. In the southern states before the Civil War, the yule log was found and chopped down by slaves. It was then brought back to the main house and set ablaze by the owners of the land. As long as the log continued to burn, the masters paid the slaves for all labor performed on the property. Hence, the larger the log, the greater the earning season for these men and women. In the days before slavery was outlawed, the yule log gave thousands of slaves their only chance at being paid for services.

Most of the rituals attached to the yule log were kept intact over the years. The only major change involved the period the felled timber was to burn. As hearths had shrunk in size, the standard time required for the ritual was carved down from twelve days to twelve hours.

The French were probably the first to dramatically alter the yule-log custom. By the eighteenth century, Frenchmen no longer burned the log. Instead, it was presented to children as the source of their gifts. The piece of timber was brought into the home and covered with a cloth. The children were to beat it with sticks and demand gifts. When the cloth was removed and no gifts were revealed, the children were forced to go outside and confess their sins. When they returned, they found gifts packed around the log.

The French eventually replaced even the gift-giving yule log with the *buche de Noel*, a log-shaped cake. It was served after midnight mass on Christmas Eve at a supper called *Le Reveillon*. Most yule logs found in today's Christmas celebrations are cakes or candies and owe their existence to the French Christmas tradition.

The wheel of time turns, and with it the passing of the seasons. As times change, many of the oldest customs are lost. Born of a pagan misunderstanding of the meanings of winter and summer, the yule log was transformed into one of the first Christian family customs. It was a tradition that warmed not just the home, but also the heart. Though this tradition never fully shed many of the superstitions that accompanied it through history, the bright light that filled the fireplaces where yule logs burned always served as a vivid reminder of the light that came to earth when Christ was born. In the few places where the yule log still glows each year, the connection with the reason for celebrating the season somehow seems stronger too.

True Stories of Inspiration and Faith That Inspired Some of the Greatest Christmas Carols, Hymns, and Popular Songs

Stories Behind the Best-Loved Songs of Christmas
Ace Collins

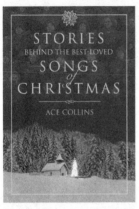

Behind the Christmas songs we love to sing lie fascinating stories that will enrich your holiday celebration. Taking you inside the nativity of over thirty favorite songs and carols, Ace Collins introduces you to people you've never met, stories you've never heard, and meanings you'd never have imagined.

The next time you and your family sing "God Rest Ye Merry Gentlemen," you'll have a new understanding of its message and popular roots. You'll discover how "Angels from the Realms of Glory," with its sublime lyrics and profound theology, helped usher in a quiet revolution in worship. You'll learn the strange history of the haunting and powerful "O Holy Night," including the song's surprising place in the history of modern communications. And you'll step inside the life of Mark Lowry and find out how he came to pen the words to the contemporary classic "Mary, Did You Know?"

From the rollicking appeal of "Jingle Bells" to the tranquil beauty of "Silent Night," the great songs of Christmas contain messages of peace, hope, and truth. Each in its own way expresses a facet of God's heart and celebrates the birth of his greatest gift to the world—Jesus, the most wonderful Christmas Song of all.

Hardcover: 978-0-310-80757-5

Pick up a copy today!

The Real Inspiration Behind the Composing of American Hymns—and
Why They Became So Important to Americans in Trying Times

Stories Behind the Hymns That Inspire America
Songs That Unite Our Nation
Ace Collins

From the moment the pilgrims landed on the shores of the New World, to the dark days following September 11, songs of faith have inspired, comforted, and rallied our beloved country. *Stories Behind the Hymns That Inspire America* describes the people, places, and events that have shaped the heart and soul of America. The stories behind these songs will fascinate you and bring new meaning and richness to special spiritual moments in the history of our nation. Discover how:

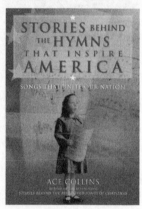

- "Faith of Our Fathers," sung at Franklin Delano Roosevelt's funeral, had its roots not with the pilgrims but with a Catholic fighting for the right to worship freely in Anglican England
- World events, from the downing of Flight 007 in Russian airspace to Desert Storm and September 11, propelled Lee Greenwood's "God Bless the U.S.A."
- Combining African rhythms and southern folk melodies, slaves brought Bible truths to life with songs such as "Roll, Jordan, Roll"

The songs in this book have energized movements, illuminated dark paths, commemorated historic events, taken the message of freedom and faith across this nation and beyond, healed broken spirits, and righted wrongs. Their stories will make you proud of your heritage as you realize anew that in America, even one voice can have a lasting influence.

Hardcover: 978-0-310-24879-8

Pick up a copy today!